Britain's Mysterious Past

BRITAIN'S MYSTERIOUS PAST

Jennifer Laing

David & Charles Newton Abbot London North Pomfret (Vt)

British Library Cataloguing in Publication Data

Laing, Jennifer
    Britain's mysterious past.
    1. Great Britain – History
    I. Title
    941   DA30
    ISBN 0–7153–7587–3

Library of Congress Catalog Card Number 78–74071

Set and printed in Great Britain
by Redwood Burn Limited, Trowbridge and Esher
for David & Charles (Publishers) Limited
Brunel House   Newton Abbot   Devon

Published in the United States of America
by David & Charles Inc
North Pomfret   Vermont 05053   USA

Contents

Introduction		7
1	Secrets of the Grave	11
2	Royal Mysteries and Murders	29
3	Giants in Chalk	42
4	Heroes and Myths from Britain's History	48
5	Castles and Citadels	67
6	Caves and Caverns	87
7	Hoaxes and Forgeries	95
8	Lost Gods, Their Supporters and Adversaries	107
9	Riddles of the Stones	120
	Appendix I Where To See Britain's Mysterious Sites	145
	Appendix II Chronology of Events	151
	Index	157

Introduction

The past is mysterious. That is one reason for the fascination it holds for man, for by its very nature most of it is lost. If we think back to our own childhood our memories play tricks, some seemingly trivial events stand out as though lit by the spotlight of the mind – every movement, every sound, every smell as vivid as they were for us then, when we were but five or six years old. Other events, which we know from various sources must have been an important part of our experience, are a total blank, a dark void that try as we will we cannot fill. To hide our confusion our minds sometimes deceive us, inventing 'experiences' we never had, dim memories of events which never happened but were a part of something read in a story-book as a child and forgotten. Psychologists tell us that the 'previous lives' experienced by some subjects under hypnosis, though vivid enough to be real for those hypnotised, are the products of the sub-conscious, 'films' created by the mind out of things read about and long since forgotten by the conscious memory. But, just as there is such a thing as a personal fantasy of the past, so too is there a national fantasy of the past, a folk-history that tells us as much about our developing country as any true history learned from the pages of history books.

Some of the gaps in human knowledge about the past are filled with myths. Some are filled with speculations, which on occasion the modern historian and archaeologist can do something towards proving or disproving. But, however convincing the explanations,

7

are they necessarily the right ones? Are they nothing more than new myths? One recent study of myth-making in our own age discovered that myths were alive and flourishing in suburbia and in the rarified atmosphere of dons' common rooms. Scientists and academics were found to be consciously or unconsciously the best fabricators of fantasy, starting off stories which were passed among other learned colleagues. These became more elaborate and were made increasingly convincing with bogus scientific jargon until they had all the appearance of fact. All too often a 'learned explanation' or simply a name is given to a phenomenon, and modern man thinks that an understanding has been reached. After the thousands of words, the many reports and analyses it is arguable whether we really know any more about such mysteries as, for example, the purpose of Stonehenge than people did hundreds of years ago. Are some of the 'myths' debunked by scientists entirely without foundation in truth? Folk tradition is amazingly persistent. As has been shown many times, truths about numerous ancient places, albeit dressed in fantasy, are handed down from generation to generation, for two thousand years or more. Was the medieval legend that the stones of Stonehenge were brought from Ireland by the magician Merlin a folk-memory of the fact that the stones were brought from a far-off land? Science has suggested that the place of origin might have been Wales, though Irish connections with Stonehenge in its final phase have been favoured by some archaeologists, who think its builders traded with Ireland. Some have even noticed Irish-style carvings on some of the stones. Consider, too, the local legend of the burial mound of Sutton Hoo in Suffolk, which was said to contain the body of a king along with a great treasure. The legend was proved to be substantially true – though the body was strangely elusive (see p 27) – over 1,200 years afterwards. However, even as new discoveries about the past come to light, legends grow up about them. The legend of the king buried with treasure in the burial mound at Lexden, Colchester, excited folklorists – until it was found to have begun *after* the excavation of the mound in 1927! A burial mound in Berkshire is called 'The

Cunning Man', but was named after the local pub, not vice versa.

Over the centuries layer upon layer of myth and mystery has grown up in the English countryside. There seems little doubt that events can leave an 'atmosphere'; one explanation put forward has been that places can 'record' particular events, which the subconscious can play back like an old film. This might explain such phrases as 'this place gives me the creeps'. Even the most cynical among us has probably experienced a 'bad atmosphere' in places, or a sense of mystery and magic.

In the following pages, some of the mysteries of Britain's past, and the 'solutions' to them that have been offered, are considered.

Map to show the location of mysterious features to be seen in Britain

I

Secrets of the Grave

As every good maker of horror-films knows, all that is required to bring the audience to the edge of their seats is a skull or two and a stone sarcophagus with its lid slightly askew. And any archaeologist will tell you that visitors to his excavations will invariably ask (after 'Have you found any gold?') 'Have you found any skeletons?' There is no way to cheat death, but the anonymity of death and ways of perpetuating memory of the individual for as long as possible have always been an obsession of the living. The man who can invent the everlasting memorial will, by his very act, ensure himself the highest honour that society can bestow on him. Many people have sought immortality; to that end men have sweated and toiled, building more and more elaborate tombs, have devised methods of preserving bodies for as long as possible after death, and carved their names on the most imperishable materials they can find in order that something of their corporeal existence shall be perpetuated.

Man's obsession with death has led to some of his finest architectural achievements: the Taj Mahal, the pyramids of Egypt, the tomb of Mausolus at Halicarnassus – one of the seven ancient wonders of the world. These are but three famous tombs, the fame of which has, ironically, outlived that of those buried in them. It is a curious fact that the only royal tomb to survive intact in Ancient Egypt was of one of the least important pharaohs (the boy-king Tutankhamun), while the last resting places of Alexander the Great or Julius Caesar are probably lost for ever.

Archaeology has shown that the homes of prehistoric man in Britain were less durable than their graves. Only a handful of settlements occupied by the first Stone Age farmers in Britain are known, in contrast to the hundreds of their burial mounds which are still such prominent features of the landscape. Much of archaeology is concerned with tombs and the dead; though the study is constantly solving some of the mysteries posed by ancient tombs, each year it brings to light new ones.

Silbury Hill

This is perhaps the most extraordinary earthen mound in Europe and undoubtedly the largest. It rises 130ft above the Wiltshire countryside, with the A361 running very close to its western side. The mystery about this mound is not *how* it was built – a problem that often perplexes modern man when observing ancient remains – but *why*. To the visitor Silbury looks not much different from the many hundreds of other ancient earthen mounds dotted around the British countryside and in most cases built as tombs for the dead. The only visible difference is that it is much larger – covering a staggering $5\frac{1}{4}$ acres. This huge monument deterred even the Romans. During the excavations of 1867 it was discovered that they had built their road from Londinium (London) to Aquae Sulis (Bath) with a detour around the Silbury mound to avoid defacing it. Since it stands so near such important prehistoric sites as Avebury Henge, it is easy to understand how as time passed it has become associated with these monuments.

The mound has excited interest and curiosity for centuries, and excavations have been carried out at Silbury on several occasions. The latest, undertaken with the most modern techniques, took place amid great publicity during 1969–70, under the patronage of the BBC. The mound certainly seemed a sensible place to dig, considering its unique size and the intriguing legends associated with it. For instance, a King Sil was said to be buried there on horseback.

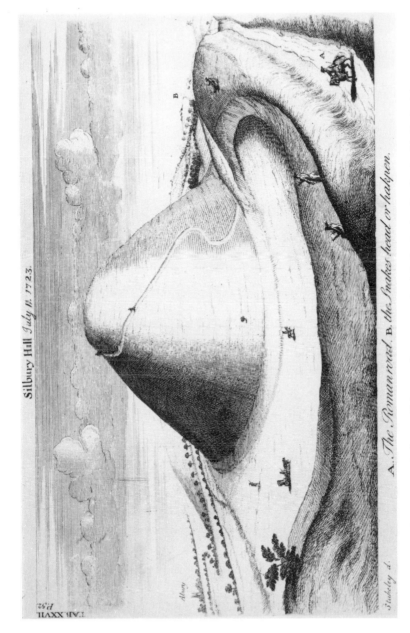

An early engraving of Silbury Hill showing the Roman road and the 'Snakes head' or 'hapken' (*Aldus Books*)

Whatever the myths about the burial, no interment came to light during the recent excavations and indeed little more was learned about it than in the first diggings of 1776, when miners dug a shaft through the mound.

The 1969–70 explorers did find a series of random boulders which do not seem to have had any function. It was discovered that ancient man had constructed the mound in three stages, probably somewhere around 2700 BC. This was during the Neolithic (New Stone Age), before metal tools were available. Workers must have used antlers as picks and bone shoulder blades as shovels. Such tools have been unearthed on other sites and experiments have shown the feasibility of these building methods. It was estimated that 50 million bucket-loads of earth must have been needed to produce Silbury.

Earth, however, was not the only material used; in the early stages turf, gravel and chalk were dumped, but towards the end the builders used only chalk, and the mound has remained durable and immovable ever since.

Owing to lack of evidence, the reason why Silbury was built has stumped archaeologists and has led naturally to the suggestion that the mound was not constructed to contain anything. Despite the absence of a burial, many experts are still inclined to the view that its intended function was probably sepulchral – though, as it would have taken a force of 500 men fifteen years to build, this would certainly be no ordinary tomb.

Other functions have been suggested for the mound. Some have expressed the view that King Sil refers not to a person but to a sun cult. The close proximity of Stonehenge and Avebury Henge, which have associations with sun worship or with calculations based on the sun's movements, might give some credence to this opinion. It has also been suggested that the hill is a giant sundial. A suggestion of a more mundane nature is that it was a signalling tower – but, if this were true, why did the Stone Age people build it so large?

The hill is one where psychometrists claim to obtain strong vibrations; one explanation has been put forward that this was a place of

Aerial view of Silbury Hill earthmound (*Aerofilms*)

such great evil that the only method of removing the horrors would have been to cover it up.

Human Sacrifice and Cannibalism

The Brenig Valley is a particularly unspoilt and picturesque part of North Wales, where the Brenig river flows gently to join the Dee. Here it was decided to make a new reservoir to regulate the flow of the lower reaches of the Dee; this would serve as the focal point of a country park which, it was hoped, would attract tourists away from overcrowded Snowdonia.

In 1976, in advance of the construction of the dam, archaeologists carried out a number of rescue excavations, giving particular attention to a series of Bronze Age burial mounds (barrows). The most complex of these burial mounds was one known rather prosaically as Brenig 45, which lay in the centre of the cemetery. It was found that, after the first burial had been made and the mound heaped up, other burials had been dug into the side of the tumulus. One of these was a cremation, deposited in an urn which had been set on the edge – a common custom. There was nothing common about the remains inside the urn, however; they comprised the earbones and two molar crowns of an infant, the rest of the body being absent.

Had this been a unique discovery, it might have been regarded simply as a curiosity; but on the island of Anglesey similar findings of infant earbones had been noted. The first was at Bedd Branwen (Branwen's Grave) – Branwen was a character in medieval Welsh legend – where three pairs of petrous temporal bones from newborn babies were found burnt. The excavator, Miss Frances Lynch, supposed that, as these are harder than most bones, they were all that had survived of the skull in a cremation. When she came to excavate at Treiorwerh, also on the island, she found the earbones of a six-year-old child. The skull of a six-year-old would certainly survive cremation, so here was proof that the earbones had been specially selected for burial.

These are the only authenticated records of earbone burials in Britain, though other suspected cases are known from elsewhere in North Wales and Yorkshire.

The conclusion is difficult to escape. The earbones are found deeply embedded in the brain, and to remove them would involve removing the brain. It is probable that in Bronze Age Britain infants were sacrificed, and their brains ripped out, the bones being buried separately as symbols of the brain. Possibly, as in some other primitive societies, the brain was eaten.

Human sacrifice is difficult to prove from archaeological evidence, cannibalism even more so. Apart from the human burials in some of the ritual pits of Iron Age and Roman Britain, the remains of a partly dismembered child were found during excavations in the Iron Age fort of Wandlebury, near Cambridge, and a human torso and limbs in an Iron Age pit at Danebury, Hampshire. Although there could be other explanations for these finds, it seems plausible that they might be the gruesome relics of cannibalism.

Did They Die for Love?

In 1959 some workmen were building the foundations for a new farmhouse at Sewerby, near Bridlington, in Humberside, when they came upon some human teeth and some beads. The police were called in, but experts were able to convince them that these were not the remains of a murder victim – at least not a modern one.

Archaeologists took over, and made a grisly discovery. In the filling of a large pit, 7ft long, they came upon a skeleton of a female adult, with face and hands down, elbows up and feet high. Across the backbone was a large corn-grinding stone. From the twisted position of the skeleton it was plain what had happened: the young woman had been thrown into the pit alive, then, when she started to struggle, the stone was thrown down on her to stop her from getting up, and the pit was filled in. She had been buried alive – but why? As the archaeologists dug down, they found the answer. Beneath the murdered woman was a burial – of an elderly and very rich woman, who had died probably in the seventh century. The girl, probably a slave, had been killed to accompany her to the afterlife.

Such bizarre finds are not uncommon. More recently a skeleton of a young woman was found in an Anglo-Saxon grave at Winnall, in Hampshire. Once again the evidence was fairly clear – she had been murdered. Experts believe that she met her gruesome fate because she had been raped. In Anglo-Saxon times, rape victims were shown no sympathy, but were regarded with contempt.

The Vikings also adhered to the custom of burying women to accompany their men to the afterlife. One such case of suttee, as it is called, was found at Ballatreare, in the Isle of Man. Here a Viking leader was laid to rest in a wooden coffin in a mound composed of turves from all over his farm lands. In this instance, the end was slightly less agonised for the female victim, for the back of her skull had been sliced off with a sword. A similar type of Viking burial was found at Westness on the Isle of Rousay, Orkney, in 1968.

Such burials serve to emphasise how little is understood of life and beliefs only twelve or thirteen centuries ago.

The Mystery of Maes Howe

The vast mound of Maes Howe rises abruptly from the flat Orcadian landscape, its stone portal – like some fairy entrance to an underground treasurehouse – betraying nothing of what lies beyond. In the heart of this earth-covered dome, 24ft high and 115ft across, is the finest example of prehistoric architecture in north-west Europe.

It is not so much the size of Maes Howe as the skill of its construction which amazes the modern visitor. To crawl down the 36ft-long entrance passage, with its damp smooth walls and floor, is like making a journey into the distant past. A torch on a long, snaking electric cable faintly illuminates the cavernous interior, with its walling

Maes Howe burial mound showing the central chamber (*Department of the Environment*)

of massive stone blocks. These are so carefully cut that it is impossible to insert a knife blade between them, yet each weighs up to 3 tons. Small slivers of stone have been placed here and there to level individual blocks, while others have been meticulously rebated to fit exactly the corner of an adjoining stone. No mortar was used and though there are indications that some stones were finally dressed with metal chisels – at a time when metal must have been extremely rare in the Northern Isles – most were fashioned entirely by means of stone mauls and hammers.

The central chamber is 15ft square, with a corbelled vault rising in the form of a dome. The passage enters at one side, and in each of the other three walls is an opening into a smaller chamber. When construction had been completed, the entrance was sealed by cunningly sliding a block into a recess in the passage wall. The whole structure was then incorporated into the mound, which was contained by revetment walls – these are now hidden in the mound itself.

In the central chamber time has stood still. The huge blocking stones to the openings of the smaller chambers lie as if wrested away by a giant hand. No wonder the Vikings were filled with fear when they first investigated this prehistoric edifice on their arrival in the Northern Isles! To them it was *Orkahaugr*, the 'howe' or burial mound of some long dead chief, whose treasure was no doubt guarded by a malicious creature intent on destroying any who might disturb it. Yet, in the twelfth century, break into it they did – and left their graffiti for later generations to decipher. One inscription tells how Norse Crusaders broke into the mound to shelter from a storm, and that one of their party went mad and ran out into the night. According to another: 'Hakon single-handed bore treasure from the howe'. Was this wishful thinking? Did the Vikings find anything except crumbling bones and a few worthless scraps of pottery?

When the mound was opened by antiquaries in 1861 they found nothing, not even a bone or a fragment of pottery. The great mound offered no clue as to its origin. Although Maes Howe is the best of the Orkney tombs, there are, fortunately for archaeology, other similar

Wayland's Smithy in Oxfordshire – a classic example of a chambered tomb (*Janet & Colin Bord*)

examples that have not been so plundered. Here the fragments of pottery and stone tools indicate that the people who built Maes Howe were Late Stone Age farmers, living in Orkney about 4,000 years ago. Scientists have also learned that, when Maes Howe was built, the landscape was very different from that of today and would have been much more wooded.

Like Silbury Hill, Maes Howe was obviously erected with some purpose. What this was, and why it was so ruthlessly cleaned out, remains a mystery. Although it must have been intended as a tomb – since it fits into the series of Stone Age burial places built between 3500 and 2000 BC – why were no interments found within it? Was it

Kit's Coty House, near Aylesford in Kent. Now denuded of its mound, the stones of this tomb are still very impressive (*Janet & Colin Bord*)

built for one man or was it, as seems likely, the family vault of a local clan chief? Was the howe the masterpiece of a great prehistoric architect, or the outcome of a team effort? And lastly, did the Vikings really find gold inside? Since gold sun discs were found in a slightly later mound at the Knowes of Trotty, it is not impossible that an appropriately finer treasure originally lay within Maes Howe.

Journey to the Centre of the Earth?

Archaeologists investigating a prehistoric burial mound at Normanton Gorse, Wilsford, Wiltshire, in 1960, noticed the weathered top of what looked like a very deep pit or well and began to clear it out. It soon became apparent that it was in fact a shaft, which had silted up naturally. It was obviously very ancient, for a pit dug into the top of the filling contained Roman and later fragments of pottery, while at a depth of 9ft a piece of Iron Age pottery was found, dating perhaps to the second or third century BC. After clearing out the uppermost infilling of silts, the archaeologists encountered a deliberate filling of chalk rubble and flints.

The shaft had been discovered in the high summer; with the onset of winter it was apparent that the excavators would need to return the following season. Just before the expedition packed up, however, some fragments of Middle Bronze Age pottery were found in the fill of the shaft, at a depth of about 40ft. This proved that it had been used during the period. Up to this point digging had been carried out with the aid of serial ladders and a mechanical hoist, but obviously more specialised equipment would be needed to clear out the shaft to any greater depth.

In 1961 the archaeologists were back, equipped this time for a major operation. Lighting was laid on, along with an air supply (in case of concentrations of carbon dioxide) and a telephone for communication with the surface. A pump was also provided to keep the shaft dry. By the end of 1961, the diggers had, despite considerable difficulties, reached a depth of over 80ft. They had by now encountered water-logged conditions, but were rewarded by more finds: a Bronze Age shale ring, some worked wood and further fragments of Bronze Age pottery.

Another season of work, in 1962, was aided by a more powerful pump. The diggers emptied out mud, the trip to the bottom of the shaft and back again by then taking 15 minutes. Communication was improved by the introduction of closed-circuit television. Much time was saved since the supervisor on the surface could direct the digging at the bottom by watching his screen, and was able to take photographs direct from the television picture. As the shaft was a mere 6ft in diameter only two people could work in it at one time.

The bottom was reached at 100ft. The walls and floor showed the marks left by antler picks – clearly the shaft was unfinished, perhaps owing to a water-bearing fault being encountered in the chalk. The sides of the shaft had been cut back with a broad-bladed axe and, where seams of flint had been crossed, the flint had been neatly severed and trimmed.

At the bottom of the shaft a variety of wooden articles were found, including the staves and bottoms of tubs, a hod-like container and a bowl. Other finds were a length of rope, a bone needle and some pins, and a number of ornate amber beads.

Two questions needed to be answered. How did the prehistoric engineers manage to dig such a shaft, and what was its purpose? The finds showed it to have been dug in the Middle Bronze Age, perhaps around 1600 BC, as suggested by a radiocarbon date from the wood discovered at the bottom. Clearly the shaft had been dug in sections; though each of these tended to go 'out of true', any irregularity in alignment was corrected in the next. The beginning of each part seems to have been checked with a template and plumb-bob. Nowhere in the shaft were there signs of foot-holds of beams, and the only way the spoil could have been removed was with the aid of some kind of winching gear.

As for its function, no satisfactory suggestion has been put forward. Its situation in association with a burial site implies that it was dug for some religious purpose – and it was the practice in some ancient religions to dig pits where offerings were made to the gods of the underworld. While there are ancient wells of similar depth to the Wilsford Shaft, none is known from prehistoric times. Other pits dating back to the Iron Age and Roman period, although not as deep, have yielded some macabre finds which serve to illuminate the world of ancient man.

Of comparable Bronze Age date to the Wilsford Shaft was one excavated at Swanwick, in Hampshire. This was not a well but something constructed as part of a grisly prehistoric ritual. At the bottom a stake had been packed around with clay. In the lower part of the shaft

SECRETS OF THE GRAVE

the walls were coated with a rich, brown deposit which analysis showed was originally flesh and blood.

Of the Iron Age and Roman pits and wells, almost a hundred have been discovered. Some are undoubtedly wells, originally dug to ensure a supply of fresh water but adapted at some stage to serve more sinister purposes. At Greenhithe, Kent, three human skeletons had been set side by side at the bottom of a well. At Newstead, a Roman legionary fortress in the Borders, Scotland, excavators at the beginning of this century found large numbers of ritual pits, one of which contained the skeleton of a dwarf. In another, human bones had been buried 'standing' upright with a spear nearby.

Dogs too were popular gifts to the gods of the underworld, as were hares and cocks and the skulls of ravens. Inanimate offerings included hazel nuts and acorns (perhaps symbols of rebirth), knives, spears and swords — the latter sometimes bent to release their 'spirit'.

Many of these offerings are known to be sacred to the ancient Celts. Julius Caesar in his *Gallic War* mentions that hares and cocks were venerated by the Celts, and there is abundant evidence that ravens were considered magical creatures. Oak trees were regarded as sacred by the Druids, and oak branches as well as acorns have been found in these strange pits.

The similarity between the shafts at Wilsford and Swanwick and the shafts and wells of the Iron Age have led some archaeologists to conclude that the Druids may have been the priests of a religion far older than was once supposed. It is possible that the beliefs of the Iron Age Celts go back not merely to the Bronze Age but to the New Stone Age, and as such are a part of the very fabric of prehistoric Europe.

Holes in Their Heads?

Trephining, or trepanning, is a surgical operation of quite considerable antiquity. It entails cutting a piece of bone out of the skull to expose the brain. Surgeons carry out the operation for a variety of reasons, mostly in order to effect delicate brain surgery, such as the removal of a tumour. But it is a constant source of mystery why such a hazardous operation should have been carried out in ancient times and, considering the medical resources then available, how it was done. In many societies headaches and other disorders were thought to be induced by evil spirits entering the brain, and therefore a hole had to be made to let them out. In some cases it was thought necessary to reduce pressure on the inside of the skull, while in other instances more magical reasons may have prevailed, since the removed roundels were used as charms.

It appears that in the remote past a remarkable number of trephined people survived their ordeal. Numerous skulls have been found in which the surgical incisions had healed, suggesting that the victims had lived to a ripe old age. Some of the earliest date to the Neolithic period. A good example was found at Crichel Down in Dorset in 1938, where a Beaker Period burial in a round barrow had a skull broken by a round hole. The removed roundel had been placed with the body and had presumably been carried round as an amulet in life.

One of the most interesting groups of trephined skulls has come from Anglo-Saxon cemeteries in East Anglia, datable to the sixth century AD. Four skulls were found, each cut in a distinctive manner. The expert who examined them pronounced that the people had been operated on by the same surgeon, for the method of making the incisions was unmistakable – all being eliptical instead of the usual circle or square. All had been made with the same instrument – probably a bronze chisel, used to gouge slivers of bone from the ever-deepening channel. The surgeon was no butcher; all four operations had apparently been completely successful, and did not result in later infection, as was usually the case. To have achieved this result the 'master of the Gliding Gouge', as he has been called, would have had to be extremely skilful, and prepared to deal with profuse bleeding and potential danger. How he managed such a feat is still a mystery.

Sutton Hoo: The Case of the Missing Body

A tomb built in the early seventh century AD – at the time when trepanning was common in Anglo-Saxon England – was discovered at Sutton Hoo in Suffolk, in 1939. It was the greatest treasure hoard ever to come to light from British soil. The original ownership of the contents, and whether or not a body was buried with them, are matters of dispute.

The discovery of a great cache of gold and silver as though out of an Arabian Nights' Tale is always fascinating. Undoubtedly the man for whom the Sutton Hoo jewels were made would have appeared a splendid figure to his Anglo-Saxon warrior followers, as the gold and garnet encrusted shoulder clasps, sword pommel and baldric mounts glinted in the sun. He would have addressed them wearing the regalia of a magnificent barbarian prince. Perhaps he wore this finery when receiving diplomatic gifts from foreign lands – such as the great silver dish, made in the imperial workshops at Constantinople for the Emperor Anastasius (AD 491–518), which was found in his grave. Were the Byzantine silver bowls and other exotic silverwork, the bronze vessel from Egypt, the coins from Merovingian France all sent as gifts to a princeling of a barbarian, uncivilised country? Or had they been obtained through negotiations and trade, as status symbols for the king of this small East Anglian realm?

There were other mysteries posed by the discovery of this remarkable grave. In the chamber of the mound, within the great ship in which the treasures had been buried, were two spoons, marked SAULOS and PAULOS in Greek. Such objects were commonly given to Christian converts; they refer to the conversion of Saul on the road to Damascus, after which he took the name of Paul. Could it be that these spoons were in the possession of the king because he had been converted? Yet it was not usual for Christians to be buried with worldly goods, for they were irrelevant in the Kingdom of Heaven; and this was certainly a burial in true pagan tradition, for the king was being sent off with all the luxuries and necessities of life.

The mound, which by tradition marked the burial of a king and which resembled other grave mounds of the period in Britain and Scandinavia, contained no body. For thirty years scholars argued over the implications. Some suggested that the king was indeed a Christian and had been converted despite his followers, who still adhered to the old ways and gave him a pagan 'burial'. Others maintained that he had been lost at sea – a possibility that might seem to be corroborated by the fact he was 'buried' in a ship and must therefore have belonged to a sea-going community.

Could any clue to his identity be found from history? If so, history might provide an explanation for the absence of a body. This fortunately was a period when some rulers' names were recorded, for it was in the early seventh century that the Anglo-Saxon ancestors of the English began to adopt writing and started to make historical notes about themselves. A king called Raedwald, one of the Wuffingas of East Anglia, seemed a likely candidate for the Sutton Hoo burial. He was great enough to be afforded such honours, and he is known to have been converted, whilst his kingdom lapsed into paganism after only a short period of Christianity. He died about 624 or 625, a date compatible with the type of objects found in the grave. Scholarly opinion now tends towards accepting Raedwald as the mysterious king who was buried in the Sutton Hoo ship, if buried he was. It is now thought that his body may well have been in the ship but that the acid conditions of the sandy mound may have removed it without trace. Forensic tests were not conclusive and the mound remains much of a mystery.

2

Royal Mysteries and Murders

Places associated with the royal family always have a special significance in the minds of their subjects, and any mystery or dark deed associated with royalty exerts a particular fascination. Often the true events surrounding royal individuals have been obscured over the centuries, either because of misleading propaganda or simply because the facts have been lost. A number of places have acquired a reputation in the popular imagination as being secretive and sometimes forbidding.

The Tower of London

One of the first places a visitor to Britain will wish to see is the Tower of London, the resting place of the Crown Jewels and the residence of the Beefeaters or Yeoman Warders whose picturesque Tudor costumes delight the tourists. The fortress is also a place of mystery and intrigue, guarding some of the darkest secrets in British history. Folk traditions have it that the Tower was founded by Julius Caesar; this is extremely unlikely, though Caesar's campaigns did take him near the site in the first century BC. Part of the wall of the later Roman defences can be seen adjacent on Tower Hill; the ruins of the Wardrobe Tower stand on top of a Roman bastion, with a 10ft-long section of Roman wall behind.

(*Overleaf*) The Tower of London, a stronghold that guards some of the darkest secrets in British history (*Aerofilms*)

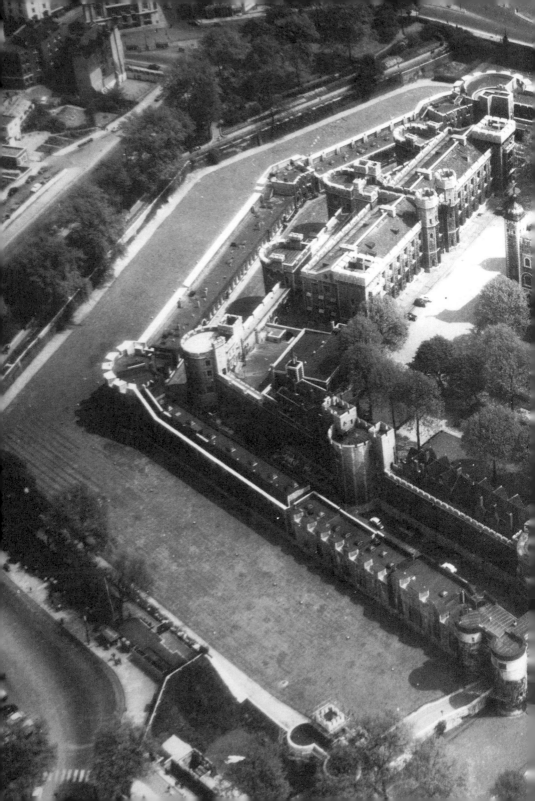

As it stands today, the keep – the White Tower – was built in the eleventh century by William the Conqueror. The enclosure erected round the White Tower in 1066–7 was enlarged, probably in the time of Richard the Lionheart (1189–99), and the present Bell Tower constructed in the south-west corner. During the reign of Henry III, the enclosure was further elaborated (1216–72), the tower now known as the Bloody Tower serving as a water gate to the Thames. The final development was left to Edward I (1272–1307); among other elaborations, he added the Beauchamp Tower and what became known as Traitor's Gate.

It was not without reason that the Bloody Tower got its name. Its walls represented the end of the road for many famous and infamous people, among them the tragic and romantic figure of Lady Jane Grey who was beheaded only minutes after her husband.

Perhaps the most widely known of all the Tower's prisoners were the two children now familiar as the Princes in the Tower. It was a tumultuous period at the end of the Wars of the Roses. On his deathbed Edward IV had given his two young sons, Edward – the heir to the throne – and Richard, into the protectorship of their uncle Richard, Duke of Gloucester. Known as Crouchback (hunchback), he was a man maligned by many and revered by others as misunderstood. Richard eventually secured the throne himself on the grounds that the two boys were illegitimate. Edward V, the twelve-year-old king, and his young brother were imprisoned in the Bloody Tower. Were they killed or not? If his claim was legitimate, Richard III would have had little need to murder the young princes, yet assassinated they seem to have been.

In the early years of the sixteenth century Sir Thomas More – who himself ended up in the Tower – wrote an involved story describing how Richard III sent a message to the Constable of the Tower telling him to give the keys to the Tower to one Sir James Tyrell for a single night. The two children were then smothered and put under the foot of the stairs beneath a heap of stones. The bodies, according to More, were later removed, though he did not say where they were taken.

More describes this event as a confession by Sir James Tyrell, and his story caused problems of interpretation to historians, who doubted its reliability.

Apparent confirmation of the account, however, came in 1674 when workmen were demolishing a staircase outside the White Tower. In a wooden chest were the skeletons of two children — presumably the remains of the young princes who died nearly two centuries before.

It is rare in such cases for the evidence to survive long enough to be examined under modern scientific conditions, but in 1933 the bones were examined medically. It was concluded that the children were about ten and twelve years old, which tallies with the age of the young princes. It was also discovered that the elder child was suffering from a disease of the jaw; this might well have accounted for the depression from which — according to More — Edward V was suffering.

The mystery, however, remains unsolved, for the two skeletons cannot be proven to be those of the royal children. Nor is there any evidence of the identity of the supposed murderer. Some historians maintain that Richard III, the archetypal wicked uncle, had the princes put to death, as More suggests; others place the blame on his successor, Henry VII, the first of the great Tudor monarchs, while there are also suggestions that the deed should be attributed to the Duke of Buckingham and was carried out without the knowledge of Richard III.

The Screams in Berkeley Castle

Another young monarch who came to an unfortunate end was Edward II. As a baby he had been proclaimed the first Prince of Wales — held high above the battlements of Caernarvon Castle by his illustrious father, the conqueror of Wales. Edward, far from being a worthy successor, grew into a lover of frivolity and his reign was marred by the discontent of the barons. In 1314, when he invaded

Berkeley Castle – the room in which Edward II was murdered (*British Tourist Authority*)

Scotland to put down the revolt of Robert the Bruce (see p 93), he was defeated at Bannockburn.

Edward was deposed by his wife Isabella and her lover Mortimer, who fostered the idea that the king was not only mentally deficient but also a homosexual. He was then imprisoned in Kenilworth Castle. In 1327 the fourteen-year-old Duke of Aquitaine was proclaimed King Edward III.

However, the deposed king's gaoler, Henry of Lancaster, was discovered to be too lax, and Edward was given into the care of Thomas, Lord of Berkeley Castle, and Sir John Maltravers. Since Berkeley had married a daughter of Mortimer, and Maltravers had married a sister of Berkeley, these two could not have been better chosen by the enemies of Edward. By this time Isabella and Mortimer were living in open adultery, and a popular reaction resulted in Edward's rescue and brief sojourn in Corfe Castle. A second attempt to release him was foiled and Sir Thomas Gurney was sent to despatch Edward for good. It was announced from Berkeley Castle that the ex-king had died peacefully, a natural death, on 21 September 1327.

But had he? A record in the *Baker Chronicle* relates that a message had been sent in Latin, deliberately ambiguous so that it could be translated in two different ways. 'Do not slay Edward, it is a good thing to be afraid' or 'Do not fear to slay Edward, it is a good thing'. This however is almost certainly fiction. The unfortunate king's demise is traditionally attributed to having a 'hoote broche putte thro' the secret place posteriale', so that there were no obvious traces of murder upon the corpse. Not surprisingly, in view of such a horrible death, the screams of the dying man were said to have been audible to the townsfolk through the thick walls, and are supposed to be heard to this day.

An alternative tradition says that he was imprisoned in a tiny cell made foul by deadly odours, and would have died earlier were it not for his strong constitution. The cell still exists, a dank place even to this day. The mystery did not fade away with the lavish funeral two months later, for it was said that Edward had survived. His unpopular half-brother, the Earl of Kent, eventually ended up on the scaffold as a result of this rumour.

Berkeley Castle, where Edward was imprisoned, is a massive stronghold overlooking the river Severn. The keep, dungeon and curtain wall were started in the twelfth century and the great hall was added in 1340. Visitors can see, in addition to many fine works of art, the cell in which the king was supposedly murdered. The 'foul odours' which failed to kill him — so that he had to be more rapidly despatched — probably came from a deep well built into the walls; carcasses of animals and men were supposedly thrown into it.

Blood at Corfe Castle

Every Shrove Tuesday at Corfe Castle, in Dorset, the Freemen of the Ancient Order of the Purbeck Marblers hold court to initiate new Freemen and uphold their traditions, for the locally quarried limestone known as Purbeck Marble has been famous since Roman times. Corfe Castle has witnessed some stirring events in English history. It was a favourite retreat of King John, and during the Civil War experienced a particularly famous siege and 'vicious slighting' by the forces of Oliver Cromwell. Its ruined keep dates from the time of Henry I (1100–35), but most of it is the work of the thirteenth century, like so many of the great castles of England. Long before the castle was built, however, Corfe was the scene of a royal murder. In the year 978 – a thousand years before this book was written – Edward, king of all England and son of King Edgar, was murdered – but why?

Although Edward was later given the epithet of 'Martyr', he did not die for any discernible religious reason. His step-mother was in residence at the royal palace at Corfe when, according to the accounts, the sixteen-year-old king rode up to the gate and called for a cup of wine. While he chatted amicably to his kinfolk and the congregating people, the peace was shattered by the sudden emergence from the crowd of a man who seemed to stumble against the king. His horse, startled, reared up, unseating the king, whose foot was caught in the stirrup. Before anyone could do anything to prevent it, the horse bolted, dragging the young man after it, his body beaten on the stony ground. By the time the horse was caught, Edward's face was battered beyond recognition, and the finders of his body took fright and ran off. By the next day the corpse had disappeared and no amount of searching revealed it. Months passed and Edward's young step-brother, Ethelred, was crowned king, and his step-mother became the queen mother.

The mystery of Edward's death was eventually unravelled for, at a

Corfe Castle (*Department of the Environment*)

certain spot on the road from Corfe to Wareham, miracles were reported to have occurred. St Dunstan, Bishop of Winchester and one
of the leading churchmen of his day, went to investigate these strange
happenings. He found a grave containing the body of the king, mir-
aculously preserved. A knife wound could be seen in the stomach,
and this was taken as proof that the person who had stumbled against
the king, as he sat convivially drinking his last cup of wine in the
dusk, must have been his assassin. Who was it who killed Edward the
Martyr, and why? The riddle remains unsolved.

King John's Treasure

A story of lost treasure is connected with King John, the monarch
forced by his barons to put his mark on Magna Carta at Runnymede
in 1215. This celebrated charter re-affirmed the rights of the Church
and guarded against infringements of feudal custom, as well as acting
as a check on maladministration and extortion by officials.

The legendary treasure is supposed to have fallen into the Wash,
the large inlet where the rivers Welland, Ouse and Witham disgorge
into the North Sea. According to tradition, the king and his army,
along with his baggage train, were crossing the Nene estuary when
horses and men were sucked into oblivion – presumably in the quick-
sands that were common in the area at the time. Apparently engulfed
were not only documents but all the things for which the king had
most regard – the royal wardrobe and regalia, the royal chapel relics
and dozens of gold and silver objects, flagons, basins, and candelabra.

The treasure has apparently never been discovered or recovered,
despite many attempts, including some by medieval monks who carried out a rudimentary investigation of the supposed site. As is common with such stories, the location of the loss varies with each
different version. Some relate that the baggage train was crossing the
Nene estuary, but others maintain that the disaster occurred at the
mouth of the Welland – the confusion arising from the fact that the
old names for these rivers were similar.

The most reasonable reconstruction of the incident seems to be that the king set out to travel from King's Lynn to Wisbech, where he spent the night, and then sent the baggage train by a quicker but more dangerous route than the one he himself followed for the rest of his journey. The king would thus have been safe, while the baggage train crossed the river between Cross Keys and Long Sutton, and it is here that the disaster occurred. Whether this is what happened, or whether the jewels were recovered in secret, or whether the treasure was lost at all may never be known.

Was Mary Queen of Scots a Murderess?

There is no more romantic or tragic figure in Britain's history than Mary, Queen of Scots, who succeeded to the Scottish crown in 1542 in her infancy, and was executed for treason by order of Elizabeth I at Fotheringay Castle in 1587. Her story begins not in Scotland but in England. Henry VIII declared himself head of the Church of England and, being politically if not at heart a Protestant, then decided to secure his position by ensuring a Protestant marriage between his son (later Edward VI) and Mary, the infant queen of Scotland. Mary's Regent, the Earl of Arran, was a Protestant, and agreed to the match, but Mary's mother, the Roman Catholic Mary of Lorraine, did not approve of the arrangement. To settle the matter, Henry sent the Earl of Hertford into Scotland, where he sacked Edinburgh, Leith and a number of coastal villages before being beaten at Ancrum Moor in 1545. The 'Rough Wooing', as it was called, flared up into a full-scale war between Scotland and England, which continued after Henry's death.

Meanwhile, Mary had been sent by her mother to France, where she was betrothed to the Dauphin, Francis, whom she married when she was sixteen. Eventually he was crowned Francis II, and Mary became queen of both Scotland and France. When he died two years later, Mary returned to a now Protestant Scotland, where her mother had been acting as regent.

Holyrood Palace, Edinburgh (*Scottish Tourist Board*)

Mary took up residence in Holyrood Palace in Edinburgh, and there set about establishing Roman Catholics in positions of power, despite the stormings of the Protestant leader of the day, John Knox. She married a Catholic, Lord Darnley, but he proved weak and ineffectual. Mary took an interest in an Italian minstrel, Rizzio, of whom Darnley naturally grew jealous. The Protestants also hated the Italian, believing he had been sent by the Pope to help reintroduce Catholicism to Scotland.

One night 500 horsemen arrived at Holyrood Palace, led by Lord Ruthven. He entered Mary's room, using a key which could only have been given him by Darnley. Here he found Mary with Rizzio, Darnley and some others. Darnley feigned surprise, but Ruthven seized Rizzio, who clung pathetically to Mary's robes. Despite her efforts to shield him, he was dragged from the room and stabbed to death. (A plate on the floor in Holyrood House today marks the spot where he perished.) Mary was distraught: 'I shall study revenge,' she declared.

The son born to Mary in 1566 – who was to become James VI of Scotland and I of England – was believed by many to be not Darnley's but the bastard of her lover, the Earl of Bothwell. When Darnley fell ill in Glasgow, Mary went to fetch him and lodged him in a house in the Kirk o' Fields (now the site of the main building of Edinburgh University). Mary stayed in Holyrood, but made a great display of being re-united with Darnley, visiting him every day. Meanwhile, the rooms beneath Darnley's chamber were stocked with gunpowder and, when the time was ripe, the house was blown up

Was Darnley's murder the work of Bothwell, or did Mary have a hand in it? She held a 'trial' of Bothwell, at which he was found 'not guilty'. But was he? Or had Mary herself organised it, as part of her 'study of revenge'? The question is as much a puzzle now as it was at the time of the event.

3

Giants in Chalk

The wicked giant is a popular image from fairy stories, but where does such a character originate? Ever since the Anglo-Saxons came to Britain and saw the vast ruins of what had once been Roman forts, the people of these islands have been intrigued by the idea that giants once roamed the countryside. It is likely that the first stories about giants go back even farther, and were devised by the prehistoric Celts to explain the Stone Age and Bronze Age megalithic tombs and stone circles in many parts of Britain. Tales of giants were certainly popular with the Anglo-Saxons.

The notion that there was a period in the past when Britain was occupied by a race of giants was made popular by the medieval chronicler Geoffrey of Monmouth. In the twelfth century, he suggested that these fierce beings were ousted by the followers of Brutus, the grandson of Aeneas, who left Troy after its downfall.

Gogmagog

In Geoffrey of Monmouth's story, one of Brutus' followers, Corineus, famed for his skill as a wrestler, was given the West Country, where there was a high proportion of giants among the inhabitants. Here the Trojans came face to face with an army of the huge creatures, led by the biggest and fiercest of them all, Gogmagog. The Trojans successfully killed all but Gogmagog, who fought desperately with Corineus before being flung over the cliffs to his death.

Sometimes Gogmagog has been split into two, as it were, to become a pair of giants, Gog and Magog. The legend is commemorated in the Gog Magog hills rising from the flat plain of Cambridgeshire; these round hillocks are the highest points of land eastwards to the Urals. Early man saw their vantage and strategic importance. They are crowned by some nearly ploughed-out prehistoric burial mounds where archaeologists have discovered the remains of an Early Iron Age fort. Wandlebury Camp is an impressive sight; though its contours are hidden by trees, the 15 acres of the fort are still well defined by its 14ft-deep ditch. It may have been from this stronghold that Bouddica (Boadicea) launched her campaigns against the Romans and it was later a Roman encampment. So say historical and archaeological sources.

According to legend, however, these hills were once ruled by a mysterious rider who was seen only at night. His rule was supreme until one day a knight who was quartered in Cambridge – only 4 miles to the south-east and clearly visible from Wandlebury – challenged the rider with the words 'Knight to knight come forth'. The ruler then rode out on his midnight-black horse and a great struggle ensued. The knight succeeded in unseating his opponent, whose black horse was captured and taken to Cambridge. The ruler of the Gog Magog hills retained some of his legendary reputation by wounding the victorious knight with his lance. By the morning the horse had disappeared and every year, on the battle anniversary, the knight's wounds reopened.

Wandlebury has produced some mysteries of its own for the archaeologist's spade to uncover. It is one of the few excavated Iron Age hillforts to have produced some evidence of human sacrifice – or at least the cavalier treatment of the dead – for a child's legless body was found in a pit where it had been thrown in a sack or cloth.

In 1954 the well-known archaeologist and occultist T. C. Lethbridge, while excavating at Wandlebury, uncovered the outline of a man's head and possibly two animals cut into the chalk. The meaning of these scribings – in some ways reminiscent of designs on Celtic

43

coins of the first century BC/first century AD – is difficult to guess. They have now been covered over again.

The Cerne Giant

Many of the massive carvings cut into the turf of chalky hillsides in southern England – mostly white horses or regimental insignia – originated during the last two centuries, but a few are very much older. One of the most ancient and widely known is the Cerne Giant, an impressive 180ft-tall figure outlined in chalk on a hill above the village of Cerne Abbas in Dorset. This giant, remarkable for his unprudish display of manhood, is almost certainly connected with fertility rites. Although he brandishes a club above his head, his appearance is not fearsome. Since the name Helith has been attributed to him, it has been suggested that he is Hercules, the Roman demi-god famous for his feats of strength – the Labours of Hercules. In that case, the giant may have been carved in the fourth century AD. Once the focus of May Day festivities, an enclosure can be seen to his left and above him where the maypole was erected. His association with fertility is kept alive by the superstition that if a barren woman spends a night sleeping on the giant's body she will be able to bear children.

It has been suggested that the Cerne Giant was one of several figures and that Hercules (or Helith) is to be associated with Gogmagog. Another legend relates that the Cerne figure represents a Danish giant who led an invasion of Britain. Unfortunately he fell asleep on the hillside; the local villagers cut off his head and drew a line round him to warn off other Danish raiders.

The Long Man of Wilmington

Another chalk-cut giant is the Long Man of Wilmington, carved from the turf on the north side of Windover Hill in East Sussex. The

The Cerne Giant, 180ft high, carved into the hillside at Cerne Abbas in Dorset (*Aerofilms*)

The Long Man of Wilmington (*Aerofilms*)

earliest accounts of this figure suggest that he dates from as late as the Middle Ages; in his present shape, he is the product of re-cutting in the nineteenth century. He stands holding a shaft in each hand — or, according to another theory, he may be opening a door.

A clue to the Long Man's identity emerged during the excavation of an Anglo-Saxon cemetery at Finglesham in Kent in 1964. Here a buckle came to light decorated with a figure holding two spears, naked except for a belt and a helmet, which had serpent-headed horns. The important feature about both the figure on the Finglesham buckle and the Long Man is that in each case the feet are turned sideways — a trick of Dark Age art. The Finglesham Man represents the Germanic war-god Woden or Odin, and it is possible that the Long Man was a similar representation, altered and made less warlike owing to the influence of Christianity. He may therefore have been cut as early as the seventh century, but no-one can be sure of his exact age.

4

Heroes and Myths from Britain's History

There are two kinds of history: what in days gone by used to be called 'authentik' and the legendary variety – romantic tales that find a place in school books despite the fact that there is no authority for them in written records of the time. Some of these stories have arisen out of the elaboration of actual events; others could have happened but probably did not, while yet others certainly did not happen. All are of interest because they shed light on past attitudes towards personages who did live and events that did occur. British history is full of these myths: King Alfred and the cakes, King Arthur and his knights, Robert Bruce and the spider, King Canute and the waves. A special category of tales concerns legendary heroes – the champions of popular causes who may have been no more than petty criminals in the eyes of the state.

Robin Hood

Sherwood Forest is a place full of meaning for any schoolchild. It conjures up visions of bands of intrepid outlaws, who lived by their wits and strength, ambushing the Sheriff of Nottingham's men or any rich passer-by to earn their living and assist the deserving poor. The 'Merry Men' – notably Friar Tuck, Little John, Will Scarlett – are as indelibly printed in the memory as their leader, Robin Hood, that most famous of all legendary English characters. The tales, which were created in medieval times, acquired further elaboration in successive periods – Maid Marian being added to provide feminine interest. But did Robin Hood exist and, if so, was he anything more than a common bandit?

Legend does not give the reason for his being outlawed, but he is said to have been 'of yeoman stock'. He is first mentioned in a poem by William Langland, *The Vision of Piers Plowman*, which was written down in 1377. The only indication as to his identity lies in his being called Robin of Loxley – a place supposedly in Yorkshire, though there is another of that name in Staffordshire. Unless Robin was fairly mobile, fleeing from one haunt to another, neither location gives any clue to why he was most often associated with Sherwood Forest – now little more than a large wood near Nottingham.

Robin of Loxley is supposed to have lived in the time of the unfortunate Edward II (see p 33). One story relates how the king, curious to hear more of this outlaw who had defied so many of his lawmen, disguised himself as an abbot and found his way to the robbers' den. When his identity was discovered, he pardoned Robin and the outlaw was taken to live at court. However, the life of uncertainty and freedom in the forests proved too great a lure, and when he was allowed a week to return to his old haunts Robin never came back to civilisation. Twenty-two years later he fell ill and made his way to Kirklees Abbey – now Kirklees Park – whose prioress was said to have been his aunt. She seems to have bled him over-zealously, however; with his dying breath, Robin managed to blow his horn, summoning Little John, his right-hand man, from the forest. Taking up bow and arrow, Robin shot an arrow out of the open window and asked to be buried where it fell. A mound in Kirklees Park is traditionally taken to be the burial place of Britain's most persistent and evocative legend.

Lady Godiva

One of England's most famous folk tales is that of Lady Godiva and Peeping Tom. To shame her husband for his harsh cruelty to the people of Coventry in the Middle Ages, the lady is reputed to have ridden naked through the streets – hidden by her long hair. All the inhabitants, except Peeping Tom, are supposed to have locked themselves indoors so they did not see her pass by. For his voyeurism, Tom was struck blind. Until 1962, a carnival Lady Godiva, dressed in rather more than her birthday suit, annually rode through the streets of Coventry to keep alive the tradition. But how did the legend start? Was there a real Lady Godiva?

Just before the Norman Conquest Earl Leofric of Mercia, along with three others, ruled England under the Danish King Cnut (Canute). Leofric's wife was Lady Godgifu, who died in 1067. She seems to have been a wise and virtuous lady, in contrast to her husband. At this period the English were being forced to pay taxes to the Danes, and Leofric was assiduous in extracting dues from his subjects.

The accounts of Lady Godiva's deed vary as time goes on – the earliest surviving version being written down in the twelfth century. It might well be that she did not ride through the streets naked but merely without her badges of office. For a great lady of that period this would have been equally shameful and certainly a fitting penance for her husband's misdeeds.

Leofric is reported to have been so taken aback by her action that he exempted the town from paying the *heregild* tax (*here,* an army; *gild,* a tax); he also stopped persecuting the Church. Evidence of this may be found in Stow church in Lincolnshire, which contains impressive arches from the Anglo-Saxon period. It is known from a charter that Leofric and Godiva gave gifts to the church in 1055 to help support a college of canons at Stow which had been founded by Bishop Eadnoth of Dorchester.

The story of Peeping Tom was not current until several centuries later, however, but it caught the popular imagination and Coventry now has a statue of him to remind visitors of the legend.

Wild Edric of the Marches

The Marcher Lands bordering England and Wales have always been a mysterious, turbulent region – separating people of Celtic origins and the Anglo-Saxons. Until the modern boundaries were drawn there was never a real barrier between the two regions, though Offa's and Wat's Dyke served to demarcate the no-man's land. Standing on the heights above Shrewsbury on a stormy day can be an overwhelming experience to anyone brought up in towns, because of the sheer remoteness and hostility of the natural environment. It is not surprising, therefore, that the figure of Wild Edric should be reported riding furiously across the wilds. He was seen, for instance, by a man and his daughter at Minsterley, Salop, on the eve of the Crimean War, for Wild Edric is supposed to appear whenever England is in danger. He appeared again in 1914 and in 1939 before World War II.

Edric is unusual in that he is a known historical personage – he is mentioned in the Domesday Book as holding lands and, in 1067, was a leader of anti-Norman agitation in the area. He and the rebels who followed him were successful in many parts of the countryside, and finally threatened the Norman garrison at Hereford. Two years later he led the sack of Shrewsbury. It is not known why he made peace with his enemies, but two years afterwards he had ceased his rebellious activities and within two more years was to be found taking part in the Norman campaigns in Scotland. Although there is no further record of Edric, legend relates that for his treacherous peacemaking with the Normans he was prevented from dying and was destined to haunt the lead mines of Shropshire for eternity. It is said that he can be heard when a rich lead vein is nearby, though his most useful attribute must be his warnings of war.

Wild Edric was married – so legend but not history tells us – to the beautiful fairy, Godda. One version of the myths about him says he was not forced to haunt the mines but died of a broken heart. She had arrived home after an unexplained absence and, when he confronted her in fury, she simply disappeared.

Hereward the Wake

Perhaps Hereward the Wake's best claim to immortality lies in the perpetuation of the myth about him by Charles Kingsley in his novel. But Hereward was a folk hero long before Kingsley wrote about him and, like Wild Edric, he fought against the Normans.

There is no doubt about Hereward's historicity. A contemporary account of some of his activities survives in the *Anglo-Saxon Chronicle*, which describes how in 1069 he used the appointment of Turold, an unpopular abbot of Peterborough Abbey, as an excuse to destroy the town and loot the church. As far as can be established, Hereward was a Lincolnshire landowner who owed allegiance to the abbot of Peterborough. It seems that his lands were seized by the Normans, which accounted for his actions. Both Anglo-Saxons and Danes rallied round his standard; after the sack of Peterborough he hid at Ely in the heart of the Fens and waited for the reprisal. It was not slow in coming. William the Conqueror had to build a causeway across the marshes from Aldreth, establishing – so the story goes – a witch in a timber tower to utter curses and spells to weaken the morale of Hereward's army. Hereward beat off the attack by burning the causeway – and, incidentally, the witch with it. Not until 1071 was Ely taken, probably by treachery, but Hereward escaped. Nothing is known of him further from history, though traditionally he harried the Normans a while longer before being reconciled to William, who gave back his lands.

Like all good folk heroes, Hereward had various supernatural trappings added to his legendary adventures; accounts abounded of his fight with a fairy bear and a Cornish giant, and of his travels in Flanders where he supposedly acquired a magic suit of armour.

Joseph of Arimathea

It is said that Joseph of Arimathea, after placing Jesus' body in his tomb, took up the Holy Grail – the cup used at the Last Supper – and

The Chalice Well, Glastonbury (*Janet & Colin Bord*)

The Chalice Well spring (*Janet & Colin Bord*)

came to Britain, where he hid the vessel in the spring which now feeds the Chalice Well at Glastonbury, in Somerset. This tradition, almost certainly invented by the monks in the twelfth century to enhance the reputation of their abbey, has persisted down the centuries, establishing Glastonbury as a place of mystery and supernatural powers. The waters of the Chalice Well were renowned for their healing qualities – possibly the scientific explanation would be their high mineral content – but the Grail supposedly contained a few drops of Christ's blood which would explain the source of the superstition.

According to legend, Joseph had previously visited Britain, trading for tin, and had been accompanied by Jesus as a young boy. Joseph is said to have struck his staff into the ground on top of the hill known as Weary-All. The stick took root and flourished into the Holy Thorn. The botanical name for this is *Crataegus oxyacantha*, and it flourishes in several places in Glastonbury, notably near the ruins of the abbey. The original thorn was destroyed in the time of Cromwell, on the grounds that it was an idol.

The Grail's Last Resting Place?

Rosslyn Chapel, founded in 1446, lies near Roslin in Lothian, Scotland. It holds a secret that has not been unravelled to this day. In the very ornate building, originally intended as part of a proposed collegiate church, stands a pillar, elaborately carved with remarkable intricacy. In the heart of this, according to tradition, the Holy Grail was laid to rest. This legend is difficult to substantiate without destroying the pillar, but the judicious use of metal detectors has indicated that there *is* something metallic inside.

There is another story concerning this column, known as the *Prentice Pillar* – Prentice being an abbreviation for apprentice. The master

The Prentice Pillar, Roslin, traditionally believed to contain the Holy Grail (*Scottish Tourist Board*)

mason responsible for most of the work in the chapel is said to have planned a pillar but, lacking the expertise to complete it, decided to go to Italy to study architecture and gain insight and inspiration. In his absence the design for the pillar was revealed in a dream to his apprentice, who thereupon set about carving it. On his return, the master mason saw the pillar and, enraged at the young man's skill and arrogance, struck him dead with a mallet. The reconsecration crosses, that were necessary after the desecration of the chapel by this deed, can still be seen.

King Arthur

There are more places associated with King Arthur than with any of England's folk heroes. In the West Country in particular, people will point out Dozmary Pool — not, in fact, bottomless as it was said to be — where Arthur's sword Excalibur was taken by a hand rising from the water. At Tintagel you may be shown the castle where Arthur was born — though it was not begun until the twelfth century — and the cave in which he was brought up by Merlin, the magician (the rocky, beautiful headland was occupied in the time of the historical Arthur). Then, another attraction at Glastonbury in Somerset is the site where Arthur and his queen Guinevere are reputed to be buried. According to other versions of the legend, however, he is still alive — but sleeping until his country needs him; there are numerous hills under which he is supposed to slumber. Among the contenders for the site of his great battle of Mons Badonicus are Liddington Castle, in Berkshire, and Badbury Rings, in Dorset. And across the length and breadth of the land there are ancient prehistoric chambered tombs or standing stones erroneously associated with him, such as Arthur's Quoit in Cornwall. As for King Arthur's round table, a fourteenth-century wooden version is on display in Winchester, while earthworks claiming to be it may be seen at Caerleon, in South Wales, and in Cumbria.

Who was King Arthur? For a long time it was thought he never existed, but the current view is that he was a leader of the Britons

Tintagel Castle, Cornwall (*Robert Estall*)

around the beginning of the sixth century, when they were fighting
the Anglo-Saxon invaders.

The Arthur that Britons know and love is a figment of the medieval romantic imagination. The most famous account of the king was
written in the 1130s by Geoffrey of Monmouth. According to his *History of the Kings of Britain*, Arthur was the son of King Uther Pendra-
gon, and Yverne (Igerna), the wife of Gorlois, king of Cornwall –
the product of an adulterous affair brought about by Merlin. At the
age of fifteen, Arthur drew his sword Caliburn (Excalibur in later
accounts) from the stone where it had been set in such a way that it
could not be removed by anyone except himself. He was then
crowned king at Silchester, and took up arms against the Saxons,
defeating them at Mount Badon – which Geoffrey of Monmouth
locates near Bath. In Geoffrey's account, Arthur then married Guinevere, and became the conqueror of the Orkneys, Norway, France
and Iceland. With his court at Caerleon-upon-Usk in South Wales,

Badbury Rings, Dorset – one of several possible sites for Arthur's great battle of Mons Badonicus (*Aerofilms*)

according to later tradition he set up his famous round table where nobody should have precedence over anyone else. Here sat the knights, who had come from all over the land to serve their king. They had to prove themselves in battle three times before they were deemed worthy of the ladies of the court. Fine manners, costumes and games were features of this legendary court – and astrologers, including Merlin. Among the many knights were Sir Lancelot, who won the love of Guinevere from the king, and Sir Galahad, who led the search for the Holy Grail (see p 54).

Arthur then went to Gaul, where he defeated the Roman emperor Lucius. He was going on to Rome but, hearing that, in his absence, his nephew Modred had allied with the Saxons, Arthur was forced to return to Britain. In the battle fought at Camlann, Modred was killed by Arthur, who was himself mortally wounded. The king was taken to the Isle of Avalon – usually associated with Glastonbury – where he was tended by queens, though his death was not witnessed.

The basic legend was elaborated by medieval minstrels, who added various subsidiary themes, such as the story of Sir Lancelot and the quest for the Holy Grail. An important cycle of Arthurian romances was made up in France by Chrétien de Troyes. In the fifteenth century all the legends were gathered together by Sir Thomas Malory in his *Morte d'Arthur*, which had the distinction of being printed by William Caxton, printer of the first books in England. In the nineteenth century, during a new wave of romanticism, Arthur became popular with the pre-Raphaelites and such romantic poets as Tennyson, who wrote the *Idylls of the King*.

Historically, Arthur is known only from some notes – intended to help in the calculation of the date of Easter – which appear in a ninth-century compilation, usually ascribed to Nennius, a Welsh monk. The entry for the year 518 says: 'The Battle of Badon in which Arthur carried the Cross of our Lord Jesus Christ on his shoulders for three days and nights and the Britons were victorious.'

For 539 the entry reads: 'The strife of Camlann in which Arthur and Modred perished, and there was plague in Britain and Ireland.'

To these meagre records can be added a few others from historical sources. Arthur appears to have been a leader of the British resistance to the Anglo-Saxons in the last years of the fifth century and the early years of the sixth. Although not mentioning Arthur by name, the writer Gildas mentions the battle of Mons Badonicus as taking place in the year of his birth, and asserts that since that time Britain had been free from external attack. The exact date of Mons Badonicus is a matter of dispute; many think it should be perhaps as early as 495. There is no reason to believe the battle was not a real event, for there

South Cadbury Castle, Somerset, the possible site of Camelot (*Janet & Colin Bord*)

is some evidence to suggest that for a while, in the first half of the sixth century, the Anglo-Saxon advance westwards was halted.

What kind of a person was Arthur? After the Romans withdrew their forces from Britain in the early years of the fifth century, Roman life continued in the towns at least for a century or more. Before their departure, local administrations had apparently been set up under the guidance of Roman officials, or prefects – a process not unlike modern devolution. Such administration continued for some time in Roman guise, the local leaders assuming Roman titles and, no doubt, Roman manners and institutions. As time wore on, these leaders became kings, and their administrative regions turned into kingdoms, which progressively lost their Roman characteristics and grew more and more Celtic. In Arthur's time, Roman ways had not been completely forgotten, though they were dying out. Arthur is best seen as a

Roman-style commander of a native field unit, perhaps calling himself by a Roman title, assuming a barbarian adaptation of Roman dress and tracing his line back to men with Roman names – his predecessor, for instance, was called Ambrosius Aurelianus.

A glimpse into Arthur's world can be obtained from the excavation at South Cadbury, in Somerset (see p 78). Pieced together from archaeology and history, this Arthur is very like other British leaders of the time, but he has that 'extra something' which has earned him immortality.

Boadicea

On the Thames Embankment in London stands a statue of one of the most famous women in British history – Boadicea, or Boudicca, as she is usually termed now. She was the wife of Prasutagus, king of the Iceni of Norfolk and Suffolk at the time of the Roman conquest. When the Romans moved into Iceni country during the fifties and early sixties of the first century, there was much resistance to their progress, though the might of their four legions against the disorganised Celtic Britons proved overwhelming. In AD 60 or thereabouts King Prasutagus died, leaving his estates jointly to the Roman empire and his two daughters – perhaps so that his family could continue to enjoy at least some of their comforts and possessions. His tactics were in vain, however; the Romans sent in to administer the will behaved as though they were confiscating the lands of dissenters, not accepting the gift of estates. The queen and her daughters were insulted; Boudicca was publicly flogged and her daughters raped. The Britons were infuriated by this disgrace, and Boudicca earned herself a place in history by rising up with her followers and taking the towns of St Albans, London and Colchester, killing 70,000 inhabitants. The river ran red with blood in Londinium, relates Tacitus, the Roman historian of the rebellion. The commander of the Second Legion refused to send help to the Romans, many of them veteran legionaries; some took refuge in the temple at Colchester before being slaughtered.

The statue of Boadicea on the Thames Embankment in London (*D. D. Griffiths*)

During the Roman reprisals, in AD 62, 80,000 Britons were killed; this ended the uprising and Boudicca poisoned herself. The queen was buried on the site of the battle in Londinium – by tradition her body lies under Platform 10 at King's Cross Station. Boudicca and her daughters are said to haunt the earthwork of Amesbury Bank in Epping Forest.

Did the Phoenicians Come to Britain?

Pick up any old school history book and the chances are it will have a story about Phoenician traders coming to England to obtain Cornish tin. In the pages of the *Children's Encyclopedia* the picture of rich merchants bartering with worthy ancient Cornishmen dressed in skins is hard to forget. These fulfil a desire to make the past mysterious and exciting, to show that our ancestors came from sunny, exotic climes and carried on fascinating secret trades. Despite its long life, the story of the Phoenicians visiting Britain is nothing more than an Elizabethan fable.

Who were the Phoenicians? Archaeology tells us that they were the descendants of the Canaanites of the Bible, who flourished c1000–574 BC; they were then absorbed into the Babylonian Empire, though their trading and influence continued long after that. Their homeland was in Lebanon and Syria, and here they built such famous cities as Tyre, Sidon and Byblos. Phoenician adventurers founded a colony at Carthage in North Africa, reached Tartessos in Spain and, according to tradition, circumnavigated Africa.

The way in which these Biblical people became a part of British history can be traced back to antiquarian interest in the sixteenth century. At this time there was much concern with determining the origins of nations; Trojans, Greeks, and the Lost Tribes of Israel, Noah and Japhet were all canvassed as suitable ancestors of the people of Britain. The man really responsible for introducing the Phoenicians to these islands was a certain John Twyne, headmaster of Westminster School, who died in 1581. In his posthumous *De Rebus Albionicis Britannicus atque Anglicis* (1590) he suggested that *caer*, the Welsh word for a fort, was Phoenician (in fact it comes from the Latin *castrum*), as were coracles, and the conical hats of Welsh ladies. He also put forward the idea of Phoenicians coming to Cornwall in search of tin, and the suggestion caught on. By the eighteenth century St Michael's Mount was thought to be the favoured trading place, and antiquaries vied with one another to find more and more 'evidence' for Phoenician activity.

If the Phoenicians themselves did not come to Britain, some very exotic objects were nevertheless brought in during the course of trade – perhaps by foreign traders whose origins can be detected but whose identity remains a secret of the passing years.

St Michael's Mount (*E. H. Lumb*)

The Unknown Traders Who Brought Exotica to Britain

As early as the Neolithic period (New Stone Age) beautiful polished jadeite axes were being brought to Britain from Britanny, and a figurine of a goddess reached far-off Shetland from the sunny shores of Iberia. Bronze Age trade was even more far reaching; burial mounds in Wessex have yielded small blue glazed beads of a type of earthenware usually termed faience, and similar beads have been found as far north as Scotland. Faience was an invention of the Ancient Egyptians and, though other civilised peoples of the Mediterranean also used it, analysis of the beads found in Britain suggests that they were made in Ancient Egypt during the eighteenth dynasty, *c* 1450 BC. Although other Egyptian objects have been found, it seems unlikely that the Ancient Egyptians were trading directly with these islands. It is much more probable that they were brought here from Greece by Mycenaean traders.

The Mycenaeans were a powerful people centred on the citadel of Mycenae in the Peloponnese. In the nineteenth century, the German millionaire-eccentric, Heinrich Schliemann, excavating the great shaft graves (dating from the earliest days of Mycenaean civilisation), believed he had found the golden treasures of Agamemnon and other Homeric heroes. He was not wrong, however, in recognising the greatness of the Mycenaeans, which eclipsed that of Minoan Crete from the sixteenth century BC onwards.

The Mycenaeans were great traders, whose interest in Britain is shown by a variety of objects which seem to be of Mycenaean origin found in the Wessex burial mounds. From Mycenaean graves in Greece amber beads manufactured in Britain have come to light; there is little doubt that Britain was important as an intermediary on the great amber route from Scandinavia to the Mediterranean. The pins used to fix the handle on to a dagger found in a rich burial at Bush Barrow, in Wiltshire, were made of a type of wirework developed by the Mycenaeans. The same grave contained gold ornaments and other items, showing how Mycenaean influence had penetrated this Bronze Age chieftain's world.

Of all the exotic objects imported from the Mediterranean into prehistoric Britain, none is more splendid than the Rillaton Cup. This beautiful corrugated beaker was found in 1818 in a burial mound near Rillaton Manor, in Cornwall. Local legend narrates how the mound was haunted by the ghost of a druid, who accosted passers-by and offered them a drink from his gold beaker, which could not be drained. A drunken hunter, tired of attempting to empty the cup, threw its contents in the face of the druid – and soon afterwards was found dead with his horse at the bottom of a ravine. The story is probably a nineteenth-century invention.

At the beginning of this century, Edward VII is said to have kept the Rillaton Cup in his dressing-room to hold his collar studs; as a result of discreet enquiries it subsequently found its way to the British Museum. Of Mycenaean or, less probably, Minoan manufacture, the beaker is without parallel in Europe, though a similar gold cup was found at Fritzdorf in Germany and there are a pair from one of the shaft graves at Mycenae.

The Greeks, like the Mycenaeans before them, were interested in northern Europe and in the sixth century BC began trading from their colony at Marseilles with the Celts of France and Germany. Fine Grecian treasures travelled as far north as the Iron Age Celtic fort of the Heuneburg, in south-west Germany, where the defenders imitated the Greek-type mud-brick bastions in their system of fortifications.

The Celts had a great liking for Greek wine. To drink it, the Celtic chiefs had to have the right Grecian cups and bronze mixing bowls and jugs. In exchange for wine and drinking vessels, the Celts no doubt offered such commodities as iron, salt, furs and amber. In any event, either directly or indirectly, some of these products from Greece reached Britain. The top of a decorated bronze jug of the sixth century BC was found at Minster in Kent, and other vessels, complete but less ornamental, have been unearthed elsewhere.

After the sixth century, there was a lull in the Greeks' trading with Britain, but it picked up again in the first few centuries BC. The Greek writer Poseidonius recorded that the Greeks traded for tin which they obtained at Ictis; this has been identified as St Michael's Mount in Cornwall, near the source of the tin, but was more probably the Isle of Wight. Several hundred Greek coins of the earliest centuries BC have been found in Britain – two of them, both in Hampshire, in Iron Age excavations.

At the beginning of this century, three Greek pots were found together in an artificial cave at Teignmouth, in Devon. The dating of Hellenistic pottery of the fourth century BC was not then well advanced, so they are unlikely to have been placed there as a hoax. Could they perhaps have been a votive offering to the gods left by a sailor blown off course, some Greek Sinbad? We can only guess, but in view of the other evidence it is not unlikely.

5

Castles and Citadels

At once gruesome and romantic, conveying simultaneous images of colourful pageantry, of feasting and carousing, and of cold, running walls, castles have come to symbolise the Middle Ages, the era of chivalry, knights in shining armour, damsels in distress, and prisoners tortured horribly in rat-infested dungeons.

It is true that the Middle Ages were the golden era of castle building. Fortresses were developed in the eleventh century in response to a particular way of life; warfare was of fundamental importance and social structure depended on the feudal system, a complicated scheme of personal ties in which land was given in return for military service.

Such castles were by no means the first defensive structures to be built. Almost as soon as man settled down to farm and fish he needed protection for his stock and from his enemies. By *c*1000 BC complicated hill-top forts were being constructed, with ramparts of earth and stone, sometimes reinforced by timber. These hillforts were to dominate the European landscape from the Bronze Age through the Iron Age; some were still being used and even built in the centuries after the collapse of the Roman Empire. The Romans constructed forts and fortresses of playing-card shape with ranges of internal buildings. It was William the Conqueror who introduced the castle proper into Britain, the characteristic Norman version comprising a *donjon*, or tall keep, within a walled enclosure. During the thirteenth century there were various developments in castle building to counter the tricks of besieging armies.

The advent of firearms and gunpowder in the fourteenth century gradually led to such fortresses becoming obsolete. They could be taken fairly easily with cannon, and warfare became a more mobile and less static pursuit. By the sixteenth century more luxurious accommodation of the type provided by Renaissance palaces was coming into favour, though many old castles remained in use. Over the centuries, these fortified buildings have witnessed barbarous atrocities, hiding within their walls mysteries which to this day are unexplained.

Brochs – Scotland's Oldest Castles

The brochs, or round stone towers, to be seen in northern Scotland and the Northern and Western Isles, some attaining a height of over 40ft, were built without windows; a single, narrow door gives access to a passage, where even a fairly short man must stoop, and which is sometimes flanked by guard chambers. Inside you find yourself in a central courtyard open to the sky, perhaps with a central weed-choked well or the stone slabs of partitions of huts built within the broch long after it had fallen into decay. Who built these towers and why? Until very recently antiquaries could only guess, and even now there are many puzzles about the brochs and their builders that give rise to vigorous and heated debate.

You would need to go to Sardinia to see anything similar to a Scottish broch, and it could be argued that you would be better off staying in Britain for, though the *nuraghi* of Sardinia are older by quite a few centuries, they have a certain starkness that the unrelated and mellower brochs do not possess.

What are brochs? The name comes from the Norse word for 'fort'. They seem to have been built for the first time in the late second century BC, most of them being erected during the first century BC and first century AD. In Scottish folklore they are sometimes called Piet's Hooses (Picts' Houses), but they were, in fact, abandoned and ruined a century or more before the Picts make their appearance in history.

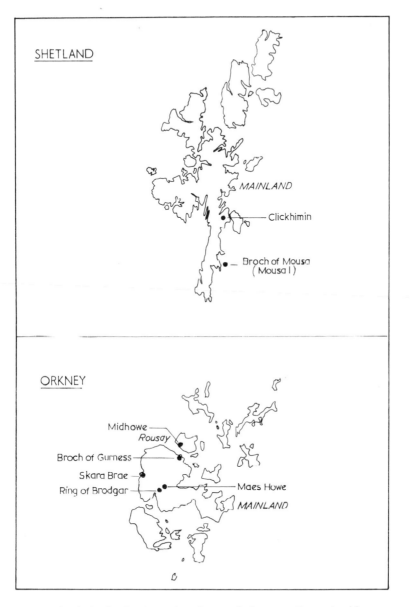

SHETLAND

MAINLAND

● ——— Clickhimin

● — Broch of Mousa
(Mousa I)

ORKNEY

Midhowe ———
Rousay
Broch of Gurness ———
Skara Brae ———
Ring of Brodgar ———

● — Maes Howe

MAINLAND

Maps of the Shetland and Orkney isles indicating the location of 'mysterious' features

69

Mousa Broch, Shetland Isles (*Department of the Environment*)

Although some – like the Broch of Mousa on a remote islet in Shetland – are still standing at an impressive height, most were not so tall and are now thick stumps of walls, perhaps 10ft high, or mounds of tumbled stones with the curve of a wall face to be seen here and there amid the moss and heather.

It has been suggested that these round towers were adaptations of forts in the Hebrides; their origins are, however, mysterious. From the Hebrides they spread to the Northern Isles and north mainland, where, for some unknown reason, much larger stone towers were built, sometimes with solid stone foundations instead of entirely hollow walls as in earlier times. Even the solid-based brochs had galleries running inside the walls at a higher level, and this no doubt served as a primitive form of insulation – not unlike the cavity walls of today. Inside the broch, timber ranges were built against the inner wall, and each tower had a central well.

One of the most romantic brochs is at Midhowe, on Rousay. It stands on the edge of a rocky geo – where on all but the calmest days the turbulent water sucks in and out in a frenzy – gazing out across the narrow strait separating the isle from Orkney mainland and enigmatically withholding the secrets of its builders' history. There are two brochs at Midhowe – one excavated by the famous antiquary Walter Grant between the two world wars and now consolidated by the Department of the Environment; the other on an adjacent rise, as yet unexplored. The consolidated broch, before it was cleared, looked just like this second mound. Now, on a summer or spring evening, rabbits play on the mellow orange-pink Orcadian sandstone at the edge of the geo.

Midhowe is a good place to see the characteristics of broch architecture. A stone wall, 13–19ft thick, encloses a courtyard over 30ft across, and still stands 14ft high in places. The wall is built up of 'skins' of masonry and is furnished with an intra-mural staircase and guard chambers, which are a popular haunt of adders. Beyond the tower, the landward side was defended by a double ditch, and a flight of steps led down to the sea where boats would have been moored. Like all brochs, Midhowe had only one entrance passage, blocked at one time by a stout wooden door. Within the broch, and round the outside, are the remains of stone huts built on the site after the tower was abandoned, sometime in the second century AD. A glass case covers an iron smelting hearth outside the broch.

No other broch is as fine as that of Mousa, in Shetland, but Dun Telve and Dun Troddan, at Glenelg in Inverness (about 8 miles west

Carn Liath Broch, Sutherland (*Janet & Colin Bord*)

of Shiel Bridge), Dun Carloway, on Lewis, and Dun Dornadilla, in Sutherland, all stand over 30ft high. These are in the care of the state, as are two others in Shetland — the broch at Jarlshof, where unfortunately much of the tower has been eroded by the sea, and the superb example at Clickhimin, on the outskirts of Lerwick.

Clickhimin broch stands at the end of a causeway in a loch. Here it is possible to see not only a remarkably well-preserved broch and the structures that were built after its ruin, but also the remains of a large and older stone-walled fort. At the fort entrance is a building of unknown function called the 'blockhouse'; hollow walled and with guardchambers, it shows clearly the kind of structure from which the brochs originated. In the shadow of the broch is a hut of even earlier date, complete with its quern, or grain-grinding stone.

Outside the broch, propped up at the entrance — and often missed by visitors — is a stone showing the impression of a pair of footprints. Experts believe that chiefs stood with their feet on the marks of such stones during their inauguration ceremonies. Is this some Scottish Stone of Destiny? If so, this is the earliest on record. Similar foot impressions are found in Orkney and at Dunadd, Argyll, Strathclyde (see p 124).

From the evidence of excavations at places like Midhowe and Clickhimin, a rough picture of the world of the broch builders can be pieced together. They were mainly farmers but also fishermen and whalers, and now and again went out to hunt for deer, seal or sea otter. Their tools were simple, mostly of bone and stone; they were, however, familiar with iron — as the finds at Midhowe show — and also worked bronze into things like finger rings. A grisly reminder of the times was unearthed at Aikerness on the Orkney Mainland just before World War II. The bones of two hands, severed at the wrist, had been cast on to the nearby midden. Three rings remained on a finger of one hand, and two on a finger of the other.

The brochs probably represent family farmsteads, elaborately protected from a constant threat of attack, though the fears or jealousies that prompted such aggressive acts are unknown. In many ways they

Glenelg Broch, Dun Troddan (*Department of the Environment*)

Dun Telve (*Department of the Environment*)

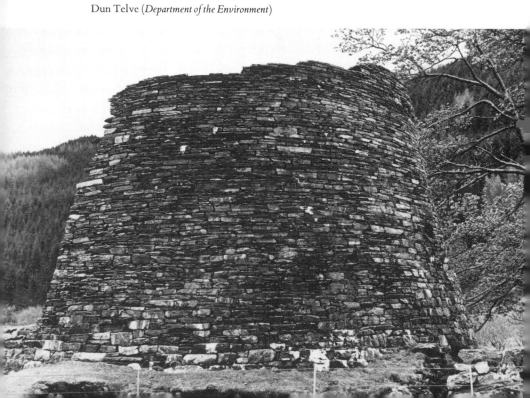

resembled the tower houses of medieval Scotland, and the grander brochs at least were very likely the homes of similar 'clan chiefs'.

There are over 300 brochs in Scotland, the majority of them in Orkney, Shetland, Caithness, Skye and the Outer Hebrides. Only ten are known to exist in the south and these must surely be outliers, built by refugees in alien countryside. The broch at Edinshall, in the Borders, is exceptionally large and is the only one of the Lowland brochs to be consolidated for the public by the Department of the Environment.

The end of the brochs is as mysterious as their beginning. During the first two centuries AD their builders seem to have had contacts with the Romans, even if these were confined to sporadic raids. Then, around AD 200, something happened – perhaps the political climate changed, perhaps the economic. Whatever the cause, the brochs fell into decay. Centuries later, when the Broch of Mousa was inhabited only by sea birds, it was to come into its own once more. According to an Icelandic saga, it provided shelter for a pair of runaway Viking lovers.

Dun Carloway Broch on the Isle of Lewis (*Department of the Environment*)

The Dark Secret of St Andrews Castle

In the quaint university town of St Andrews — famous for its golf course rather than for its violent history — stands a stark ruin. This is the castle built in the sixteenth century for the primate of Scotland — Cardinal David Beaton, a name still equated with religious intolerance and cruelty. As leader of the opposition to Scottish Reformation, he martyred many Lutheran Protestants, among them Patrick Hamilton, a priest who objected to the sale of indulgences (pardons for sins) and who married despite Church rulings on celibacy. Hamilton was burnt at the stake, but the pyre was not big enough and the flames were repeatedly put out by rain, so that it took six hours for him to perish. Another martyr was George Wishart, whose sufferings were watched by Beaton — until it was time for him to leave to attend the wedding of his own, illegitimate, daughter!

In St Andrews castle Cardinal Beaton constructed a fiendish dungeon for his Protestant prisoners. Shaped like a bottle, it was hewn out of the rock and so contrived that there was no light and no exit, for the victims were dropped in from the room above — itself a windowless prison, ventilated by a single slot that was later blocked up. The dungeon was 24ft deep; the bottom, which is uneven, being 15ft wide. Prisoners went slowly mad in the total darkness and, tradition says, when their screams were heard in the castle, they were murdered. At least one — John Roger, a black friar — was killed inside the dungeon.

Caratacus' Last Stand?

Many people know the rhyme about the ladies of the harem of King Caractacus, and know too that he — more correctly Caratacus or Caradoc — was a British chief at the time of the Roman conquest of Britain. All over Wales there are hills called Caer Caradoc (Caratacus' fort); one in particular is associated with the famous chief — the Hereford Beacon, near Colwal, in the marcher lands between Hereford and Worcester.

Hereford Beacon (*Aerofilms*)

As far as is known, Caratacus and his brother Togodumnus led the British resistance to the invading forces of the Emperor Claudius in AD 43. The Roman general Aulus Plautius and his army met the brave Celtic tribesmen somewhere in the neighbourhood of Rochester, in Kent. The Celts were defeated, but Caratacus fled westwards into Wales, to take refuge among the warlike Silures, who had no time for the Romans and their soft ways. Under his leadership, they built up their strength, and prepared to do battle with the Romans who, in AD 51, marched into Silurian country intent on conquest.

The site of the last stand of Caratacus is not known for certain.

Contemporary Roman accounts placed it in the territory of the tribe that was allied to the Silures at the time – the Ordovices of Snowdonia. It was reported that Caratacus held a strong position among steep hills, with a river in front and the route blocked with piles of stones. While the most likely location for the battle, many experts now believe, was near Caerws, it is not impossible that Hereford Beacon was the actual site. It was almost certainly occupied at the time and would have been of strategic importance to Caratacus in his dramatic last stand.

In any event, though his wife and children were captured, he himself escaped once more and fled to Queen Cartimandua of the Brigantes or Coritani.

Knowing the price of alliance with this dangerous revolutionary, Queen Cartimandua treacherously handed him over to the Romans, who took him in chains to Rome. There he was paraded through the streets as a prisoner. His ultimate fate is not known, but according to one Roman account he was set free after he had made a fine speech, pointing out that it was more to the Romans' credit to free him than to kill him. On being shown the Eternal City, he is reported to have asked: 'Why do you so greedily desire our poor hovels when you have such stately and magnificent palaces of your own?'

The Walls of Camelot

In the late 1960s, popular imagination was fired by the excavations carried out by Professor Leslie Alcock on the site of Cadbury Castle in Somerset. To the casual observer, this was a fairly ordinary Iron Age hillfort, perhaps a little larger and more impressive than most, commanding wide views as far afield as Glastonbury Tor, many miles away in the legendary Isle of Avalon. The unique aspect that brought the hordes of tourists to South Cadbury, however, was the belief that this hilltop castle was King Arthur's Camelot. It is now believed that Arthur did exist, living at the beginning of the sixth century and waging war against the Anglo-Saxons (see p 56). Archaeology suggests that he was most likely to have had as his base a refortified Iron Age encampment and Cadbury Castle was just such a site.

Its identification as Camelot did not depend simply on the fact that it was refortified in the Dark Ages. Long before this was known, men had believed this to be Camelot. The Elizabethan scholar John Leland visited it and recorded in 1542:

> At the very south ende of the chirch of South-Cadbyri standith Camallate, sumtyme a famose toun or castelle, apon a very torre or hille, wunderfully enstrengtheid by nature. In the upper parte of the coppe of the hille be 4. diches or trenches, and a balky waulle of yerth betwixt every one of them . . . Much gold, sylver and coper of the Romaine coynes hath be found there yn plouing . . . The people can telle nothing ther but that they have hard say that Arture much resortid to Camalat.

Subsequent generations of antiquaries repeated Leland's assertion that here was Camelot, but the claim was never proved.

Cadbury Camp, showing a section through the ramparts (*A. W. Worth*)

The excavations produced conclusive evidence that the Iron Age fort had been occupied, in the fifth to sixth centuries, by men who refortified the site by building a huge rampart with timber framing and a massive timber gateway. Inside this, archaeologists discovered a timber 'hall' of the same period, fragments of pottery imported from the Mediterranean, typical knives and some Anglo-Saxon jewellery. While these discoveries did not prove that this was Camelot, they did show that it had been occupied around the time of the historical King Arthur, and by someone of importance.

One very interesting fact might seem to strengthen the Camelot theory. Cadbury Castle is a very large fort, covering some 18 acres. To defend such an area, and indeed to put up the defences round the summit of the hill, would require a considerable force of men – larger than the average war band in the fifth–sixth century. Whoever defended South Cadbury must have had control of a sizeable army; if not Arthur himself, he must have been an Arthur-like figure.

It may never be known for certain if the South Cadbury site is Camelot; an inscription mentioning Arthur by name would have to turn up on the site to remove all doubt – and that is too much to expect.

The Monster of Glamis

Not far from Dundee, in the picturesque Scottish countryside, is Glamis Castle, seat of the Earls of Strathmore. This forbidding Scots-baronial pile conceals a secret – in the words of a former earl – 'of the most appalling horribleness'. The mystery, by tradition, is revealed to the heir on his twenty-first birthday, when he is taken to a room in the castle whose existence is known only to the earl and to the agent who manages the estate. None of those made party to the secret has ever disclosed it. To this day, however, the family denies that there is any such mystery.

Glamis is reputed to be the most haunted house in Scotland. Since 1372 it has been occupied by the Lyon family, later created earls of

Glamis Castle, near Dundee. The castle is reputed to contain a secret room within the walls (*Robert Estall*)

Strathmore and Kinghorne, and forebears of Queen Elizabeth, the Queen Mother. Probably a hunting lodge in the eleventh century, the main tower dates from the fifteenth century and was extensively remodelled in the seventeenth. The castle, which has associations with Mary, Queen of Scots, and is the birthplace of Princess Margaret, is noted for its fine plastered ceilings and its chapel, with painted ceilings and panelled walls. It is thought that the secret room, which has never been discovered, may be somewhere near the crypt.

An attempt was once made to identify this hidden room by hanging a towel from every window in the castle. All but one window was seen to be displaying the white cloth, but the room remained concealed within the 15ft-thick walls. It is believed that, if it exists, the knowledge of its whereabouts — and of the mystery associated with it — may have died with those members of the family who were killed in World War I.

The rumoured presence in the castle of a monster may be accounted for by the child born in October 1821 — a hideously deformed, possibly mongoloid creature. It is thought that it did not die within the month, as was recorded, but lived on, its existence concealed following the birth of a second son, who was normal and became the heir. Usually hidden in the secret room, the elder son was no doubt exercised in that part of the castle known as the Mad Earl's Walk, reputedly haunted by weird noises and ghostly forms. A creature with tiny arms and legs and huge barrel body, he is said to have lived to be 100 and died in 1921.

Glamis is also haunted by the ghost of Macbeth, who murdered King Duncan. Earl Beardie, who died 500 years ago, plays dice with the devil in another hidden room. A tongueless woman is sometimes seen rushing through the grounds, tearing at her mouth; and the ghost of a negro page sits outside one of the bedrooms.

Lost Years in British History

In the winter of AD 286–7, Britain was under the rule of the Romans. The capital city was Londinium, and the countryside was dotted with small 'county' and market towns, the capitals of the various tribes that made up the population. Along the borders that the wild, uncivilised tribes constantly raided, the army kept the province safe from barbarian attacks. Britons were enjoying a boom in prosperity — where their great-grandfathers used to live in timber and thatched houses, the wealthier of the population had built themselves splendid stone villas, and surrounded themselves with the luxuries of life: foreign wine, silks, perfumes from the orient. Rich and poor alike adhered to laws which ultimately were to develop into the modern legal system. But this, the third century after the birth of Christ, was a tumultuous period for the Empire, and the inner turmoils of the administration were reflected even in Britain, the outermost and most northerly outpost of the civilised world. During the century there had been more than fifty men who had called themselves emperor. Usurpers to the Imperial power had defeated the rightful emperors in the field, or had been proclaimed as rival rulers by the army. Most of these *coups d'état* and murders took place outside Britannia. But in the winter of 286–7 life in Britain was to change, and the province was to become totally involved with the political unrest. For the next six years, the province broke away from the Empire, under her own Imperial rule, and it is these six years in which all historical records stop. Archaeologists have dug and found little evidence for the changeover, and historians can merely make guesses: effectively six years are lost to history.

Some things are certain. The man responsible for the break was Marcus Aurelius Mausaeanus Carausius. He was a man of the people, who had risen from humble beginnings somewhere in Menapian Gaul (now Belgium). It seems that from a boy he had been brought up to 'mess about in boats', a factor which became of supreme importance in his rise to power.

One of the inevitable consequences of the economic and political upheavals had been that in Gaul bands of dissatisfied outlaws roamed around the countryside, terrorising the population. Various mopping-up operations had been attempted, and apparently the young Carausius took part in these policing activities. He eventually was given command of the Channel, and ordered to wipe out the many pirates who were making the crossing from Britain to Gaul hazardous, and whose raids on the coast were seriously jeopardising the safety of the civilian population.

The historical records are confused, but apparently Carausius was suspected of being in league with the pirates themselves. Whatever his crime may have been it is certain that the emperor Maximianus no longer held Carausius in favour, for in 286 or possibly in 287 he ordered the sailor's execution.

Carausius had little to lose: he crossed the Channel and landed in

Britannia. There is no doubt that Carausius must have been friendly with important people in Britain, and must have had the support of the legions stationed there. There is no evidence to suggest how he gained his popularity.

It seems likely that Carausius had been guilty of conniving with the pirates since he was certainly not short of funds when he arrived in Britain: the troops were notorious for following those who could pay them well.

Thus ensconced in Britain, supported by the navy and the British legions, Carausius was strong enough to proclaim himself emperor. It might be thought that Britannia, wealthy from its cornfields in the south and its slaves and mineral riches, might have been enough for this usurper from Gaul, but this was the period at which no matter how humble a man's origins might have been, he could aspire to the highest honours in the state. The boy who had grown up in fishing boats on the Belgian coast was set to become emperor of Rome.

What happened in the next two years in Britain is not known, but some clues are provided by the accounts of the period set down by the Roman historians Aurelius Victor and Eutropius. A much fuller, but probably mostly legendary, account is provided by two Scottish historians of the fourteenth and fifteenth centuries, Hector Boece and John of Fordun.

The medieval accounts record that Carausius landed not in the south but in Westmorland. He then supposedly allied with the Picts and Scots in the north, and with their support defeated the governor Quintus Bassianus near York, due to Bassianus' army being mainly composed of a pro-Carausian sector.

In 289 the official emperor, Maximianus, planned an invasion of Britain to regain the lost province. He mustered a fleet in the Low Countries, but Carausius proved the better seaman and Maximianus was defeated. In 289 some kind of uneasy peace was made with Carausius, who extended his territory to northern Gaul, where he set up a mint at Rouen.

The nature of this 'treaty' with Maximianus can only be guessed, but Carausius wasted no time in proclaiming his 'official' status by striking coins in the name of the 'co-emperors'. At this time the Empire was ruled by two emperors, one for the Eastern Provinces (Diocletian) and one for the Western (Maximianus). On one coin struck at Colchester Carausius showed the portraits of the three emperors together, side by side, with the inscription 'Carausius et Fratres Sui' ('Carausius and his Brothers'). The reverse showed a personification of Peace, and the inscription 'Pax Auggg', the triple G meaning there were three augusti or emperors enjoying peace.

Coins were a very useful medium for putting out propaganda. Carausius seems to have wasted no time in making use of them and wooing the people. In the absence of newspapers, coins were an ideal medium for political communication, and their designs were often used to put across a distorted version of the facts. Personifications were used as a kind of political 'shorthand' – each had their own attributes which made them instantly recognisable. They are valuable historical evidence in these 'lost years'.

One of Carausius' coins struck on his arrival in Britain showed the emperor being welcomed by the Province with the inscription 'Expectate Veni'. This is taken from Virgil's *Aeneid*, and is Dido's welcome to Aeneas in Carthage – Come thou long awaited! Other coins proclaimed 'Concordia Militum' (The Concord of the Army) and 'Fides Militum' (The Loyalty of the Army), suggesting that all was not well with the troops!

Some other coins of Carausius suggest that he may have held some lavish spectacle in London to commemorate his accession, no doubt to keep the masses happy.

But trouble clouds were looming. Even though the high standard of the coins and the apparent prosperity of Britain at the time would imply that Carausius' rule was as good for Britain as the later chroniclers asserted, the official emperor was gathering his resources. By this time Carausius' foe was the heir-apparent, Constantius Chlorus, who besieged him in Boulogne in 292. Carausius' power lay in his skill with ships, and Boulogne was impregnable as long as access to it was possible by sea. Constantius Chlorus built a boom across the harbour, and, deprived of supplies, the town was forced to surrender. Carausius once more was confined to Britain. For a while he held out, but in 293 he was 'treacherously murdered by, or with the connivance of, his minister Allectus'. Using a pincer movement, Constantius Chlorus met the army of Allectus near Silchester in Hampshire, and there defeated him utterly. Allectus was killed in battle or in the ensuing rout. So ended the years of oblivion in which Britannia, though still trading with the Continent, was a breakaway state and during which the life of the people is lost. Why the legions accepted Carausius, how Carausius gained so much power, why he was murdered by his finance officer and what his real objectives were are all questions that still await answers from this mysterious period of British history.

Apart from coins, archaeology has little to contribute. But some archaeologists believe that Carausius may have been responsible for building Richborough Roman fort in Kent. Certainly the still massive walls were put up at around the time of his bid for power, though other experts believe they were already ten years old at this time. They are well worth a visit, being amongst the most spectacular Roman remains in Britain.

6

Caves and Caverns

Caves hold a special fascination. They evoke memories of childhood, of long summer days spent on beaches searching for smugglers' haunts. Many a fiction has been spun round treasure hidden in caves, and undoubtedly some did hold their store of smuggled liquor or stolen jewellery. Smelling of seaweed, their walls slimy with moisture, their sandy floors a trap for picnic debris, these are the caves where traditionally prehistoric man made his uncomfortable home to which he dragged his bride by the hair, or where unkempt hermits spent their rigorous lives. Some, more romantically, are linked in legend with particular heroes from the past. How far are such traditions substantiated by science?

Did Prehistoric Man Live in Caves?

Contrary to popular belief, very few of Britain's ancient inhabitants lived in caves. Certainly the rocky caverns along the seashore would have been most unsuitable as dwelling places, even those above the tidal reaches lacking warm shelter, dryness or security. Later, prehistoric man did inhabit caves and rock shelters from time to time, but not surprisingly preferred living in structures of stone or timber.

Cave dwelling became more commonplace during the last of the four great ice ages – the Late Glacial period lasting from about 12000 to 8300 BC. For most of this vast stretch of time Britain was gripped by a sheet of ice. Its formation caused a drop in the sea level so that in effect the island became part of the continent. Men and animals crossed the landbridge at will during the intermittent warmer periods; at times there were polar bears swimming in the Thames, while Late Glacial men travelled to the far corners of England and Wales, often occupying rock shelters. Many favoured the deep underground caves found in particular in the limestone areas of the countryside. Their very names are redolent of tradition — Kent's Cavern, Badger Hole, King Arthur's Cave, Cat Hole, Aveline's Hole, Sun Hole, Thor's Cave, Robin Hood's Cave, Soldier's Cave and Mother Grundy's Parlour.

How many of these were inhabited regularly by Stone Age man, or were used mainly for long-forgotten religious observance, it is difficult to determine.

The biggest concentration of caves occupied by Late Glacial man is in one of the great beauty spots of England — Cheddar Gorge. Cliffs of limestone tower above each side of the road running through the gorge. Despite the throngs of visitors in summer, there is a primeval magic about the place, its vast natural architecture swamping the cars and tourist shops into insignificance. The caves of Cheddar are a wonderland of nature; here time stands still for a moment and allows us to come into contact with our remote prehistoric forebears who lived, made love and died to the accompaniment of the eternal music of the dripping stalactites. The occupants lived near the cave mouth, worked their rough stone tools, devoured their game — reindeer, horse, bear and boar — and sheltered behind their flickering fires from the menace of the sabre-toothed tiger, woolly rhinoceros and wolf. The area deep within the cave, where daylight never penetrated, was reserved for man to commune with his maker. At Gough's Cave, in a glass case, can be seen the skeleton of one of these early hunters, known as Cheddar Man.

A series of bizarre discoveries has come to light not far away, at Wookey Hole, one of England's most dramatic sites. Here, in a ravine of the Mendips, the river Axe cascades out of the rock face from subterranean tunnels eroded over some tens of thousands of years by the flow of water. Like grottoes cut by dwarves, these three huge stalactite-hung chambers – now floodlit – lead to an underground lake. Below its waterline, narrow tunnels lead through the limestone to other caverns. Seven of them have been explored by potholers – unfortunately with some loss of life.

Wookey Hole has tales to tell of more ancient tragedies. The caves were occupied in the Iron Age and the Roman period, as well as later. Between the first and third chambers in the dark subterranean pool, fourteen human skulls were found in 1947–9, associated with pieces of Roman pottery of the first or second century AD. The strange thing about the skulls was that all but one were of people aged between twenty-five and thirty, and at least two were female. Archaeologists ruled out the possibility that they were trophies of war, for headhunters do not normally collect girls' heads. Were they the skulls of deceased relatives, committed to the pool as a sacrifice to the god who presided over it? The ancient Celts were obsessed with the head (see p 25), believing it to be the seat of the soul. There is no doubt that the Wookey cache of skulls has some connection with a pagan ritual.

Another prehistoric tragedy came to light in Wookey Hole. In a rock fissure near the entrance the skeleton of a man was found; he had died fully equipped with knife, dagger and bill-hook. A stalagmite ball, which may have been his lucky charm to protect him from death in the cave, had obviously been of no avail. The cause of his death may have been suffocation by smoke. His body lay undetected for 2,000 years, within easy reach of the fresh air he had apparently been so urgently seeking.

The Witch of Wookey in medieval legend lived in the cave with her familiars, a goat and a kid. (It is curious that the bones of a goat and kid were found there; also abundant evidence that Iron Age farmers had tethered their goats in the cave.) The story goes that she was made wicked by having been crossed in love, and she cast spells on the local villagers. The Abbot of Glastonbury was called in to help; she tried to flee but as she did so, was sprinkled with holy water and turned to stone. There is a stalagmite in the cave with a curious resemblance to a witch and this is believed to be her.

Another legend of Wookey related how a giant conger eel over 30ft long swam up the river Severn, crashing through salmon nets and flooding the valley with his thrashings. He was diverted into the river Axe and ended up in Wookey Hole; he became trapped in an underground pool, where he remains thrashing about for ever.

In the same gorge as Wookey Hole is the Hyaena Den, discovered in the mid-nineteenth century and excavated by Professor Boyd Dawkins, one of the great Victorian cave archaeologists. It was found to contain the bones of thousands of Stone Age creatures: cave lion, cave and grizzly bear, mammoth, woolly rhinoceros, bison, Irish elk and, of course, the hyaena that gave the den its name. Some Late Glacial men, despite their unpleasant neighbours – for hyaenas had dragged all manner of carrion into the cave – had used the place as a shelter.

Did Some Hermit Saints Live in Caves?

Caves associated in legend with local saints are scattered all round Britain, particularly in the Celtic West where, in the centuries after the Roman occupation, Celtic monks hid themselves away to live a spartan existence worshipping God.

The Christian faith, which came to Britain during the Roman period, survived the turbulent years at the end of the fourth century and beginning of the fifth after the Roman armies withdrew and Britain was subjected to repeated onslaughts by Anglo-Saxons in the south and east, Picts in the north, and Irish in the west. Some Christian communities persisted in the neighbourhood of Hadrian's Wall, in parts of south and north Wales, and in Cornwall. During the fifth and sixth centuries these groups were reinforced by Christians from the eastern Mediterranean, bringing new ideas and in part responsible for spreading the Christian faith.

The early Christians of Celtic Britain were very Roman in their outlook. They organised their Church along diocesan lines, and believed in attending to the needs of existing Christian communities rather than engaging in active missionary work. While this diocesan Church was becoming established in Wales, Cornwall and southern Scotland, new ideas were already developing in Africa and Syria — monasticism being paramount among them. The first monasteries in the East Mediterranean lands were like forts, surrounded by high walls which served both to isolate the monks from the outside world and act as a defensive barrier against marauding desert tribesmen.

In the fifth century there were monasteries in the south of France, such as that of St Martin at Tours, and by the end of the century the first monastic communities may have been established in Britain. During the sixth century monasticism took hold in both Britain and Ireland, and monasteries sprang up everywhere. This was a new kind of ecclesiastical administration, in which the monastery, rather than the urban diocesan church, was the centre of a network of churches, hermitages and minor foundations.

These early monasteries, unlike those of the Middle Ages, had no overall layout; they consisted of chapels and monks' cells scattered at random within the monastic enclosure. The monks believed in poverty and simplicity; many set out from the larger monasteries to live alone in isolated hermitages. Rock stacks and remote islets were often favoured by these hermits, and so were caves.

Did St Ninian occupy the cave that bears his name at Physgill, in Dumfries and Galloway? The earliest of the Scottish saints, he was probably a Roman from Carlisle, sent out to administer to a Christian community at Whithorn. His cave looks out on one of the most picturesque beaches on the Dumfries and Galloway coast, a delightful holiday area of Scotland. Although it had always been associated with the saint, there was no real evidence for its Dark Age use until 1871, when somebody noticed a simple cross incised on the rock near the entrance. Excavations followed in 1884, revealing a succession of stone floors and pavements which had been laid down at various times in the recent past. These had covered up stone crosses carved on

St Ninian's Cave, Scotland (*Department of the Environment*)

the walls by Dark Age pilgrims. Where these had been set up, a series of cross-decorated stones was found, the earliest dating from around the seventh century, but others were of the eighth, tenth and eleventh centuries.

Another place of veneration to which later pilgrims were drawn was St Molaise's cave on the tiny Holy Island, off the coast of Arran in Western Scotland. St Molaise was an Irish cleric, usually associated with a monastery at Devenish in County Fermanagh. When the cave was excavated in 1908 extensive remains of occupation were found in it; runic inscriptions cut into the walls by Vikings in the eleventh–thirteenth centuries can still be seen.

Were the caves in fact occupied by these hermit saints? It is possible, although it cannot be proved.

Caves to Shelter Heroes?

Scotland is well endowed with caves associated with her national heroes, William Wallace and Robert Bruce. The visitor can see several where Wallace, the great patriot and forerunner of the Bruce, is said to have gone into hiding from the English.

Wallace was made of the very stuff of folk heroes. Of humble birth, he found himself caught up in the tide of the Wars of Independence, when Scotland was being oppressed by the English King Edward I. The facts and myths about Wallace were collected by a minstrel, Blind Harry, in the fifteenth century and became part of the Scottish heritage.

On one occasion, according to Blind Harry, Wallace was in residence in Lanark, and on his way to church outside the town he saw and fell in love with his future wife, Marian Braidfute (Broad Foot). Soon after he was challenged by some English soldiers for possessing an ornamented dagger; Wallace lost his temper, and a fight flared up. He managed to escape through a back door of his own house, and fled to a cave in nearby Cartland Crags. Haselryg, the English governor of Lanark, burnt down Wallace's house with his wife inside it – an act that made the Wallace take up the Scottish cause against the English. He won an overwhelming victory at Stirling Bridge in 1297, but his forces were crushed by Edward at Falkirk. In 1305 Wallace was betrayed and taken to London, where he was hanged, drawn and quartered. His head was stuck up on London Bridge, and the pieces of his body displayed at Perth, Stirling, Berwick and Newcastle.

Wallace's Cave in Cartland Crags could be visited until it became too dangerous to enter – those intrepid enough can still venture down the face of the gorge. There is another Wallace's Cave not far off at

Corhouse – hollowed out of the rock as an early nineteenth-century folly, for the benefit of tourists visiting the scenic Cora Lynn.

In many places in Scotland visitors will be shown 'the cave' where Robert Bruce is said to have watched the persistent spider that inspired him to greater efforts on behalf of the Scottish nation.

7

Hoaxes and Forgeries

One of the strongest inclinations in human nature is to 'take down a peg or two' someone who has set himself up as knowing more than everyone else, or who is posing as being better than they are. Antiquaries have always been particularly disliked for giving themselves airs of importance, and pronouncing on this or that ancient relic as being 'Middle Magdalenian III' or 'Late Predynastic' or other such terms unintelligible to the layman. Fiction is full of pompous antiquaries, and eighteenth-century humorists in particular delighted in making fun of them for expounding in learned terms on supposedly ancient sites or objects that were not ancient at all.

It is hardly surprising, therefore, that since the seventeenth century there have been a succession of forgeries – sometimes crude, sometimes very clever, the object of which has been to fool the learned world of antiquarianism and to make the victims of the hoax appear very foolish. Sometimes the perpetrator's sole objective has been the pleasure of seeing his victim discomforted, but occasionally he has had a financial aim as well. Antiquaries have always been eager to pay for rare and curious antiquities, and the rarer and more curious these are, the more money tends to change hands.

Forgeries of antiquities are not always easy to detect even today, despite all the scientific techniques that have been developed to uncover them; just as it is believed that a horrifyingly high proportion of the 'old master' paintings in the world's galleries are modern forgeries, so it is likely that many of the great treasures in the museums are not ancient. Every year more forgeries are exposed and, before we smile at the gullibility of eighteenth- and nine-teenth-century collectors, we ought to remind ourselves that in 1923 the Metropolitan Museum of Fine Art in New York bought an 'ancient Greek' bronze horse described by the greatest classical art expert of the day as 'without doubt artistically the most important object in our classical collection'. It was attributed to the Greek sculptor Kalamis; thousands of replicas were sold at the Museum and elsewhere, and it was illustrated in many books on Greek art.

Then someone in the museum noticed a line down its back which suggested it had been cast in a manner not known before the four-teenth century AD, and the investigation began. Gamma-ray ex-amination showed that it had a wire core and sand inside it – a modern technique of manufacture – and it was rejected out of hand as a twentieth-century forgery. In 1972 further tests on the horse indi-cated that it might be of ancient origin after all. It could perhaps be Classical Greek, or a fifth century AD copy, or even a replica of the 1920s – the experts cannot agree. By using thermoluminescence, a highly sophisticated technique of dating, the horse was variously dated between 3500 BC and AD 700, which would make it appear to be 'ancient', though of uncertain age. Recently, investigation of another supposed fraud – the finds at Glozel in France – has cast serious doubts on the reliability of this method of dating, so the bronze horse may be modern after all. Even science cannot always beat the forger.

Flint Jack

One of the most notorious forgers of the nineteenth century was Flint Jack, alias 'Fossil Willy', 'Cockney Bill', 'Bones', 'Shirtless' and 'Antiquarian'. His real name was Edward Simpson and he was born near Whitby in 1815. His interest in antiquities was acquired while he was employed as a servant first by Dr Young, a Whitby historian, and later by Dr Ripley, a keen fossil-hunter, whom he accompanied on his expeditions.

In 1841 Flint Jack was making his living by fossil-hunting in the Scarborough, Filey and Bridlington area. It was when he began finding flint implements at Bridlington that the idea of forgery came into his mind. He started forging flint implements when he could not find genuine specimens to meet the demands of collectors. Gradually he perfected his skill, travelling from one district to another selling his wares, moving on as each area in turn became too risky for him to continue. Scotland and Ireland proved unrewarding because, as he said, the people were 'too cannie, and the journey would hardly bear expenses'. He did not confine himself to flints; in Malton he sold a 'Roman breastplate' and in Scarborough a 'Roman milestone' he had made.

By the 1860s Flint Jack was famous. He was invited by a Professor Tennant to give a demonstration of his skill to the Geologists' Association in London. On the platform Flint Jack

> . . . undid the knots of his red handkerchief, which proved to be full of fragments of flint. He turned them over and selected a small piece, which he held, sometimes on his knee, sometimes in the palm of his hand, and gave it a few careless blows with what looked like a crooked nail. In a few minutes he had produced a small arrow-head, which he handed to a gentleman near, and went on fabricating another with a facility and rapidity which proved long practice. Soon a crowd had collected round the forger, while his fragments of flint were fast converted into different varieties of arrow-heads, and exchanged for sixpences among the audience.

Alas, Flint Jack took to drink, and his forgeries became so widely known that he could not fool sufficient people to supply him with alcohol. Yet to the end the forger was jealously proud of his work. When he heard that Sir John Evans, the greatest prehistorian of his day (and father of Sir Arthur Evans, discoverer of the Minoan civilisation), had developed the skill of making flint implements, he visited him 'as he believed he was likely to attain an equal degree of eminence with himself'.

Flint Jack had his rivals, even if Sir John was not among them. In 1855 in East Yorkshire one William Smith, alias 'Skin and Grief' or 'Snake Willy', was hard at work, while at Stoke Newington in the 1890s forgers were perfecting the skills Flint Jack had begun. As J. Stevens wrote in 1894:

The Stoke Newington forgers found out that their imitations lacked the colour, polish and general softness of feature, and the natural abrasions present on ancient specimens, the result of time, chemical changes, and friction against other stones while drifting. These imperfections they set about remedying by resorting to cunning devices, such as brushing their forgeries over with hard brushes, shaking them up in sacks with other stones and sand, and lastly, to give the definite surface stain, boiling them in saucepans with old rusty nails, fragments of iron, etc. But some observing purchasers detected these devices, and found that reboiling removed the ochreous colour of the surface, leaving the implements grey. But the forger, not to be outdone, resorted to longer boiling, having found that the greater length of time the tools were boiled the more permanent became the ochreous stain.

Lost Civilisation of the Clyde

Of all the great nineteenth-century hoax controversies, none was so hotly debated as the case of the Dumbuck and Langbank crannogs and the Dunbuie hillfort, all near the estuary of the Clyde in Scotland.

The story begins with a perfectly ordinary excavation of what appeared to be an Iron Age stone-walled hillfort at Dunbuie, near Dumbarton, by a respectable antiquary, Adam Millar, in the late nineteenth century. While excavating a midden outside the fort wall Millar came upon a strange collection of objects, all of stone, bone and shell, that were quite unlike anything known from an Iron Age fort. His conclusion took the archaeological world by storm; they were, he asserted, 'indicative of a much earlier period than post-Roman; they point to an occupation of a tribe in their Stone Age'.

Soon after Millar's discovery, some exciting finds emerged at Dumbuck, less than 2 miles away. The excavator, a Mr Donnelly, believed he was investigating a crannog – a timber hut on an artificial island, of a type built by the natives in Scotland while the Romans were occupying Britain. The Dumbuck example, however, displayed some features not encountered in other Scottish crannogs, and the leading expert of the day, Dr Robert Munro, was called in to advise. Although he was of the opinion that the Dumbuck crannog was genuine, if slightly unusual, once again objects of a type never previously encountered on a Scottish Iron Age site were discovered. The plot thickened.

In 1901, another antiquary, John Bruce, began excavating a supposed crannog in the same area, at Langbank. Again the remains were inspected by Munro, who was of the view that here was a genuine crannog of the Iron Age; the finds included a fine decorated bone comb and a penannular brooch of a type in use during the Roman occupation of Scotland. Although the crannog was just like the one at Dumbuck, here there were 'Clyde People' finds, as the objects from Dunbuie had come to be termed.

Munro had no doubts at all about the spuriousness of some of the finds from the Dunbuie and Dumbuck sites. Seen today, they seem so badly forged – ornamented as they are with childish patterns and faces – that it is inconceivable that anyone could have been taken in by them. However, in 1901, far less was known about prehistoric antiquities. Munro had written to Millar, Donnelly and Bruce expressing his doubts about their finds, and had even written to this effect in the *Glasgow Herald*, saying of the objects from Dunbuie and Dumbuck: 'Is it not of surpassing interest to find a fort on a cold, bleak hill and a stone crannog on the Clyde containing so many children's playthings, and almost nothing else?'

99

The third site, at Langbank, seemed to confirm his theories. The British Archaeological Association became party to the controversy and 'experts' ranged themselves on either side. The mystery deepened when some Neolithic figurines were reported from Portugal that bore a superficial resemblance in some respects to the Clyde finds; it became even more involved when Australian aborigine objects were produced as further evidence. Most of the leading archaeologists of the time took up pen to write about the 'Clyde Controversy', as it became known. Professor Boyd Dawkins, the famous expert on Stone Age man, examined some of the oyster shells found at Dunbuie and pronounced them to be Blue Points, peculiar to America.

In 1905 the case was laid to rest when Robert Munro published his *Archaeology and False Antiquities.* In this he set out in full the Clyde Controversy and his reasons for believing that the sites were genuine Iron Age examples which had been salted with modern fakes. But who was responsible? The problem was complicated by the fact that Dumbuck was covered with silt every twenty-four hours, so there was no normal build-up of layers which would betray any disturbance. The whole site was in effect disturbed and false finds could be planted without difficulty. The midden at Dunbuie also presented difficulties; it was simply a mound of rubbish without any stratification within it. Could it have been that some workmen were behind the fakes, or was it Donnelly, who to the bitter end seems to have been unwilling to accept that he was the victim of a hoax?

The Mysterious Piltdown Affair

One of the greatest riddles that have ever perplexed archaeologists involved a remarkable hoax. In 1908, or shortly before, a certain Charles Dawson, a solicitor in Lewes, East Sussex, noticed some brown flints in the gravel drive leading to Barkham Manor. Dawson, so he reported later, enquired about the source of the gravel and was informed that it came from a nearby quarry at Piltdown. There he asked the labourers who were removing the material for the drive to

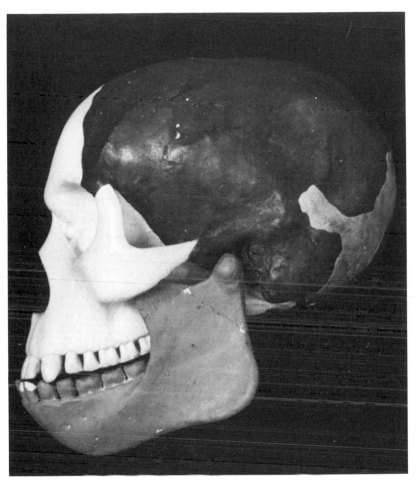

The notorious Piltdown Skull (*British Museum*)

keep a look out for bones; they said they had not so far encountered any. As a keen fossil-hunter and antiquarian, Dawson might reasonably be expected to make such a request. On a subsequent visit, the workmen produced a small piece of what looked like a 'brown coconut', maintaining they had found a much larger fragment but had broken it up and thrown the rest away. Dawson recognised the find as belonging to the left parietal bone of a skull.

The hunt was now on: Dawson became a frequent visitor to the quarry, grubbing about in the gravel in search of more fossil bones. In 1911 he unearthed part of the left frontal bone which fitted on to the fragment he already possessed. He found other skull fragments, and the premolar tooth of a fossil hippopotamus. In 1912, armed with his finds, he visited his old friend Dr Smith-Woodward, Keeper of Geology in the Natural History Museum. Smith-Woodward was flabbergasted; realising that these skull fragments might belong to the earliest man ever discovered in Britain, in May of that year he accompanied Dawson to the Piltdown gravel pit.

Dawson almost immediately unearthed the left half of a jawbone. On successive days, three pieces of cranium obligingly turned up. After a summer of digging, the two eager fossil-hunters were in possession of eight fragments of human cranium, a jawbone, nine or ten animal teeth and some crude flint implements. *Eoanthropus dawsonii*, better known to the excited world as Piltdown Man, took his bow at a meeting of the Geological Society on 18 December 1912 and remained the centre of controversy over the next forty years.

Piltdown Man was interesting for a number of reasons. To begin with, the skull's cranium looked undoubtedly human, while the jawbone seemed more like that of an ape. Could this then be the 'missing link' – the 'apeman' that marked the transition from ape to man – for which scientists had been searching almost since Darwin's day? The second question at the forefront of all Piltdown discussions was: 'How old is he?' Although his exact age was in dispute, there was no disagreement about one thing – he was the oldest human which had, as yet, been found.

In 1914 Dawson took Teilhard de Chardin, then a renowned palaeontologist, to a new site at Piltdown, some 2 miles or so from the gravel pit. Here, said Dawson, he found a molar and isolated pieces of skull among pebbles raked at the side of the field. It might have been expected that Dawson would rush to Smith-Woodward with his discovery. Instead, he kept it from his collaborator for nearly two years, reporting on it only when it became of crucial importance in assessing the evidence. In 1916 Dawson died, but the excitement engendered by his discovery did not.

After Dawson's death, arguments broke out over the relative age of the mammal fossils found with the skull and jaw. Some of them seemed much older than Piltdown Man, others about the right age. In 1949 Dr Kenneth Oakley, of the Natural History Museum – who was interested in the estimation of the age of fossils by the amount of fluorine they had absorbed from the deposit they were in – took samples of bone from the Piltdown fossils and sent them to the Laboratory of the Government Chemist for analysis of their fluorine and phosphate content.

The result was very surprising. Piltdown Man was as recent as any of the other fossils found at the site – indeed, the Piltdown fossils looked disconcertingly modern. Whatever else, Piltdown Man was far too young to be a missing link; he could be no older than the time of the last Ice Age, when man had already evolved into *Homo sapiens*.

This revelation caused many distinguished experts to look again at the Piltdown fossils. Dr J. S. Weiner, of the Department of Anatomy at Oxford University, happened to notice that the jawbone had certain curious features: the bone itself was like that of a chimpanzee, yet the teeth had been worn down like those of a human. He experimented by artificially grinding down chimpanzee teeth, and arrived at the same dentition as that of Piltdown Man.

In 1953 the Piltdown remains were subjected to rigorous scientific tests by new methods of fluorine estimation which proved that the jawbone was that of a modern chimpanzee, the canine tooth having been ground down with an abrasive and the pulp cavity filled with mineral grains. The cranium pieces were demonstrated to be old but not fossil; radiocarbon tests have since shown them to date from 500–600 years ago. The jawbone had been stained to match the skull pieces. Meanwhile, the associated fossils were examined; the hippopotamus tooth had probably been found in Malta, and the elephant fossils, which had suggested the very early dating for Piltdown Man, had come from much older deposits in Tunisia.

Piltdown Man, then, was a brilliant hoax. But who had perpetrated it, and why? Certainly Dawson seems to have been at the heart of it, and this was not his first. In 1907 he had exhibited a number of bricks from the Roman fort at Pevensey, including some bearing the stamp: HON AVG ANDRIA. Four such whole or fragmentary stamped bricks were supposedly found, of which two survive. They were taken as showing that the fort was refurbished in the reign of Honorius (AD 395–423) and, as such, provided the only evidence that the forts of the Saxon Shore, as they were called, were redefended at this time against Saxon attack. Modern tests have shown, however, that the bricks were very clever forgeries, and so another theory, followed by archaeologists for nearly half a century, has had to be abandoned. It is, of course, possible that Dawson himself was the victim of a hoax, and both Smith-Woodward and Teilhard de Chardin have at various times been implicated in a suggested conspiracy.

Richard of Cirencester

Out of the blue, one day in June 1747, an English parson resident in the picturesque town of Stamford, in Northamptonshire, received a letter from an Englishman who happened to be living in Denmark. To be fair to William Stukeley, he was no ordinary provincial vicar but one of the most remarkable antiquaries of the eighteenth century. Stukeley had given up a career as a doctor to enter the Church, and in his earlier years had been a most astute recorder of ancient remains. Stukeley's later years were clouded by an obsession with Druids (see p 108); with 'vegetable sermons', as he called them, and with a number of very silly misapprehensions – but never, throughout his varied and busy life, was he ever involved in an affair quite like that of Richard of Cirencester.

The letter he received – from a Charles Julius Bertram, apparently professor of English in the Royal Marine Academy at Copenhagen –

was full of compliments to Stukeley and his scholarship, and invited a suitably friendly reply. A warm-hearted man, Stukeley replied as one scholar to another, and in due course was introduced to the mysterious Richard of Cirencester.

According to Bertram, a Mr Gramm, a privy councillor and chief librarian to the king of Denmark, possessed certain interesting and hitherto undisclosed information about Roman Britain. Careful probing on the part of Stukeley revealed that this was derived from a medieval manuscript that had turned up in Denmark; it contained 'a history of Roman Britain, which he thought a great curiosity; and an antient map of the island annex'd'.

Stukeley left Stamford to take up a new post in London. When he had time to continue his correspondence with Bertram, it was to learn that poor Mr Gramm had died, but that fortunately a transcript of the medieval manuscript was available, along with a copy of the opening paragraphs in facsimile.

What excited Stukeley most about the manuscript was that it appeared to be based on lost Roman sources, compiled by a fourteenth-century monk, Richard of Cirencester. The most important source was an 'Itinerary' copied from the memoirs of a Roman general. Itineraries were, in effect, lists of roads marked with the distances between places, which enabled routes to be worked out. The most famous was the 'Antonine Itinerary', probably compiled in the second century. Also known to Stukeley and his contemporaries was an actual map, known as the 'Peutinger Table', compiled in the fourth century and copied in the thirteenth. There was thus nothing out of the ordinary about Richard of Cirencester's source, and the fact that he had drawn a map from it, which accompanied his text, seemed in keeping with medieval custom.

Stukeley, a careful researcher, discovered that there was such a monk as Richard of Cirencester, who had been at Westminster in the fourteenth century and had written a *Speculum Historiale de gestis Regum Angliae*. True, he had been called 'de Cirencestria', as opposed to 'Corinensis' – the Roman version of Cirencester – which was how he was known to Bertram, but that was neither here nor there. Besides, the facsimile of his opening paragraphs was clearly in a medieval hand.

Stukeley was overjoyed at his find and, with Bertram's kind permission, was allowed to read a paper about the manuscript to the Society of Antiquaries. They echoed Stukeley's joy, and Bertram was forthwith made an Honorary Fellow of the Society. In due course Stukeley brought out a book on Richard, and very soon the monk's text was accepted as a source for Romano-British studies.

Some people, however, had their doubts. The ever-sceptical Gibbon, author of *History of the Decline and Fall of the Roman Empire*, accepted Richard's authenticity while adding caustically that he showed a knowledge of Roman Britain 'very extraordinary for a monk of the fourteenth century'. In 1795 Thomas Reynolds, a noted scholar, declared his belief that the manuscript was a forgery, and by 1827 Richard was falling into disrepute. Yet even today bogus Roman place-names, derived from Richard's text, sometimes appear in local histories and occasionally on maps where they have escaped the eye of archaeologists.

Was Richard of Cirencester's manuscript really a forgery? Current opinion supports the view that it was; if so, it was undoubtedly one of the finest literary fakes of all time. The perpetrator was almost certainly Bertram; 'Mr Gramm' never existed. Bertram was not who he pretended to be; far from being a professor, he was a twenty-four-year-old student who, in the very year of his letter to Stukeley, was trying to gain admission to Copenhagen University to study history and antiquities.

8

Lost Gods, Their Supporters and Adversaries

Christianity is but one of many religions followed by the inhabitants of Britain in bygone days. Indeed, compared with the beliefs of pre-historic man, the Christian faith has so far had a short life. Beliefs explain the unknown and therefore feared, they provide their adherents with a code for living and sometimes a purpose, and they relieve the burden of human responsibility. They tend also to be surprisingly flexible (Christianity is unusual in this respect, and even Christianity has made allowances for superstition and the survival of older faiths), and can take over attributes of other religions.

Religions are essentially of the mind and spirit, and thus leave little trace archaeologically. All that can survive of ancient faiths are the remains of their temples, their cult figures and altars, and perhaps the holes they dug in the ground to receive offerings. Of the beliefs that prompted men to build the temples, erect the statues and altars, and make the offerings, no trace remains, though it is often possible to make inspired guesses. It is not surprising that past religions often assume a mantle of mystery.

Of the beliefs of Old Stone Age and Middle Stone Age man in Britain, nothing is known. Of the superstitions of Neolithic and Bronze Age Britain, more is understood, while of the Celtic religion a great deal is known though much remains a mystery. Many old Celtic beliefs persisted under the Romans – sometimes beneath a

Roman veneer – alongside the official Roman pantheon and a diversity of cults, often of Eastern origin, brought in from all over the
empire. With the coming of the Anglo-Saxons, the gods and god-
desses of northern Europe were worshipped for a while – and again
later by the Vikings in a slightly different guise – but soon pagan
beliefs were swept away by Christianity. Something of the old religions and some of the old gods of Britain survived, contributing to
magic and witchcraft in later ages. These superstitions are frequently
perpetuated in beliefs about natural phenomena of the countryside.

The Myth of the Druids

The Druids – the priestly class of the ancient Celts whose grisly rituals
disgusted Roman writers – have long been a source of mystery and
fascination. As they handed down their knowledge by word of
mouth, no written records of their status or functions in society have
survived, only the observations of their Roman enemies. Classical
writers depicted the Druids as great men of learning, though they
were probably little more than witch doctors. Most of the information about the Druids – some of it probably a misrepresentation –
comes from the writings of Julius Caesar, who says they were judges
and teachers as well as priests. They were exempt from military service and were supposedly interested in the planets and stars. They
were highly esteemed in society, and were responsible for sacrifices –
preferably of criminals but sometimes of the innocent.

The Greek writer Strabo's description of the Druid custom of
human sacrifice is almost certainly a factual account: the victims were
stabbed in the back, while priests made divinations from their death
throes. He also relates that human and animal offerings were burned
in wicker cages. Tacitus, one of the most down-to-earth commen-
tators on barbarians, said that 'they considered it a duty to cover their
altars with the gore of captives, and to consult their deities through
human entrails'.

The myth of the Druids has been strengthened by eighteenth- and nineteenth-century romanticism. Artists of this period delighted in depicting the priests in long flowing robes, their beards caught by the wind as they stood on rocks amid wild Welsh or Scottish scenery. Sometimes artistic licence would run to a Druid in blood-spattered clothes carrying out human sacrifice, or others cutting down mistletoe with golden sickles in sacred oak groves. Partly instrumental in perpetuating the myths was the eighteenth-century antiquary William Stukeley, who contracted 'druidomania' and held fancy-dress parties. In 1754 he was referring to his friends as Druids and Druidesses, and sending them presents of oak leaves.

The religion of the Celts is now believed to have been much less formal than was previously thought. It was in essence a collection of superstitions and legends, mixed with magic and ritual. The Druids must have presided over the worship of a great diversity of local divinities, beliefs were closely connected with nature and many deities were thought to reside in pools and springs, trees, groves and mountains. The use of mistletoe at Christmas is a survival of such pagan rituals and many features of the countryside are associated with Druid practices.

Among the known sites associated with the ancient Celtic gods are the remains of a wooden temple discovered at Heathrow airport, and a similar, small rectangular temple found inside the Iron Age fort at South Cadbury, Somerset. Some Celtic gods are better known than others, having become a part of folklore. One was Llyr, later turned into King Lear, made famous by Shakespeare, and who gave his name to Leicester. Many were taken over by the Romans – such as Sul, the god worshipped at Bath, who became Sul-Minerva, and Cocidius, a war god equated with Mars.

Sacred Waters

Wishing wells are common sights in gardens – often they are not functional, having only a circular head resting on a concrete or earth base. They are still popular, but why do people make wishes at wells?

A clue to the origin of wishing wells is contained in the ritual that must be observed at them. A coin, or sometimes three, must be thrown into the water when the wish is being made. Sometimes it is necessary to walk round the well three times while wishing, sometimes three wishes are granted. Three is a magical number, important as far back as the time of the Iron Age Celts, and the custom of throwing 'offerings' into wells and making wishes is a survival of pagan cult, when offerings were made to water deities and prayers offered that they might look kindly on the supplicant.

It is hardly surprising that wells, and for that matter springs and pools, have been the centre for religious observance throughout the ages. Water is not only essential to life, it has an apparent life of its own, and the dark depths of pools and wells look as though they could harbour all manner of strange beings.

Such has been the strength of superstition, that many pagan Celtic wells were 'converted' to Christianity, their presiding deities conveniently changed into saints. Brigantia, the iron age goddess who shares her name with the Brigantes tribe, became St Brigit or St Bride in the Middle Ages. In the Hebrides it was claimed that she was the midwife to the Virgin, and she was also confused with the Irish saint of the same name, who in the sixth century was abbess of Kildare according to Irish tradition. But the Irish, too, revered Brigantia, the goddess of the arts, and Brigantia may have been worshipped at Kildare long before there was a monastery there. Another 'saint' who was conveniently converted from a pagan deity was St Anne. The St Anne commemorated in the names of British wells had no real connection with the mother of the Virgin, but took her name from Anu or Annis, a sinister Celtic deity. In British lore she ate children, and in Ireland she was worshipped as the mother of all the pagan gods.

Archaeology has produced several examples of Celtic water cults. An Early Iron Age discovery was made during the construction of a runway for a wartime airfield in Anglesey. The island was well-known from the evocative descriptions of the Roman historian Tacitus, to be an important stronghold of the Druids, who held out there against the Romans in the first century AD. There was dramatic confirmation of this in 1942 during the building operations at Llyn Cerrig Bach, for this was the site of a sacred pool into which offerings had been thrown up to the time Tacitus describes. The first find was an iron chain; for a while this was used to drag lorries out of the mud, until it was discovered to be an ancient slave gang chain. Among the 150 objects found were parts of a chariot, swords, spears, bits of a dagger, a shield boss, various horse trappings, tongs, cauldrons, a sickle, a trumpet, bronze ribbons from ash staves and currency bars. Many more items no doubt still await discovery. The earliest artefacts had probably been thrown into the pool as offerings in the second century BC, and some had come from far corners of Celtic Britain and even from Ireland.

A well dedicated to a water nymph or goddess was discovered during excavations at Carrawburgh Roman fort on Hadrian's Wall in Northumberland. This well had been revered by soldiers throughout the Roman occupation, and they had thrown a variety of offerings into it. Over 13,000 coins were recovered, as well as a rich variety of small personal objects such as brooches. The haul also included several altars dedicated to the nymph, shrine bells, broken pots and a human skull. In some parts of the Scottish Highlands even today it is customary to leave broken pots beside wells.

Many wells are believed to be invested with miraculous powers. Some are supposed to be endowed with curative properties. St Winifred's well at Holywell, near Flint (Clwyd), is one such, and has the additional merit of being 'equally propitious for Protestants and Catholics'. Winifred was a seventh-century virgin who was beheaded by her would-be lover. Her head rolled down hill from the place where she was murdered, and where it came to rest a spring gushed forth. Such a story associating a severed head with a well is not uncommon, and is a survival from pagan Celtic headhunting activities.

There is a holy well dedicated to St Madron near Madron in Cornwall, one of the richest counties in England for saints' wells.

St Madron's Well is a romantic place. It is reached by following a muddy track down which water runs like a stream even in summer. The well itself is in a leafy glade, and the trees around are festooned with bits of cloth, paper tissues, even a rubber glove left by pious visitors to the place. Nearby is an ancient chapel and 'baptistry', green with moss and approached by a stile over a low stone wall. The chapel and baptistry may date from the twelfth century, though Madron was a Dark Age saint. Almost certainly however the well which now bears his name was venerated by pagan Celts.

Mithras

One of the most fascinating cults of Roman Britain was that of the god Mithras, who rocketed to fame in 1954 with the discovery, at Walbrook in the City of London, of a temple dedicated to him. The Walbrook Mithraeum attracted more public attention than any previous British excavation. Over 80,000 people flocked to see work in progress, and even dusk did not deter the pilgrims, who demanded to see the site by floodlight. After the excavation, the building was re-erected about 60 yards north-west of its original site.

Mithraism was an eastern cult which, on account of its tough in-itiation ceremony and the rigorous demands made on its adherents, appealed to soldiers, merchants and officials in Roman Britain. Women were not allowed into its ranks; its dictates and practices shared features in common with Christianity and freemasonry. Mithras was a god of light and truth, who had received instructions from the sun-god, Sol, as to how he might bestow benefits on man-kind, and combat the powers of evil and darkness. The sun-god's messenger was the raven, who directed Mithras to steal and slaughter the primeval bull, the symbol of the life-force. Mithras dragged the bull to a cave and cut its throat; as the blood gushed from its neck, the creatures of the dark otherworld came to draw life from it – the beasts of Ahriman, the god of evil and Mithras' avowed opponent. A scorpion attacked its vitals, a snake twined round, a dog jumped to lap the blood.

Mithras was born from an egg, the symbol of eternity; in reliefs and sculptures, he is shown wearing a Phrygian pointed cap, and is often depicted amid the signs of the zodiac. Some Mithraic lore is preserved in the Zoroastrian religion of the Parsees, in a collection of lore known as the Zend-Avesta.

Because of its superficial resemblance to some aspects of Christianity Mithraism came to be hated by Christians, who thought it had been invented to ridicule them. They zealously destroyed the temples of Mithras, owing to their similarity to churches – both were basilican buildings modelled on Roman public halls. These Mithraea were intended to represent the cave where the bull was sacrificed. The worst slight of all, to the minds of Christians, was the Mithraic ritual banquet shared between Mithras and the Sun, who were waited on

The Temple of Mithras at Carrawburgh fort, Hadrian's Wall

by Mithras' attendants, Cautes and Cautapates. Justin the Martyr saw it as a 'devillish imitation' of the Holy Eucharist. A travesty, too, was the baptism by water.

In the Walbrook Mithraeum, the cult had taken on some other more familiar gods, as shown by the sculptures found there. Minerva represented intellectual wisdom; Serapis, the Egyptian god, stood for success and commercial prosperity (no doubt he was popular with the merchants!); Bacchus for moral courage, and Oceanus for power over wind and wave.

Another outstanding Mithraeum can be seen, attractively laid out, at Carrawburgh on Hadrian's Wall. Here, apart from the remains of a ritual meal, the excavators found a pit used for initiation by ordeal, in this case by entombment. In a coffin-like space under the floor of the porch, the initiate lay close to a hearth, so as to experience the great heat. In some cases the fire burned on a slab on top of the initiate. Other rites involved brandings and tortures; in one instance the emperor Commodus is said to have carried out a human sacrifice 'because something terrifying had to be done'.

The Origins of Christianity

Evidence for the earliest Christians in Britain is sparse and confusing. However, discoveries made in 1975, in a field in East Anglia, showed that Christianity was not only established but flourishing in the third century AD. A hoard of treasure was discovered by a keen treasure hunter who happened to be walking across a field at Water Newton – part of the Roman town of Durobrivae. The first find was a 'chalice' or two-handled drinking cup; then there were three bowls, two with inscriptions round the rim; a delicate and richly decorated hanging bowl, perhaps a lamp; a large shallow dish; two flagons, one complete, the other damaged by a plough; a strainer decorated with the sacred monogram of Christ, and a series of triangular plaques, again bearing the monogram, called the Chi-Rho or the Christogram. The whole hoard amounted to about 10lb of pure silver (purer than sterling), and a gold disc decorated with a Christogram.

The inscriptions are dedications from the faithful; they include one which reads: 'I honour your sacred altar, O Lord, relying on you'. Experts are inclined to the view that this was Church plate of the third century AD, perhaps buried hurriedly at the time of the persecution of Christians by the emperor Diocletian in AD 303–4. The objects, possibly made locally, may have been offerings of the type popular with pagans which were being 'dedicated' to Christ – a rare instance of pagan practice overlapping with Christian.

The Water Newton hoard, found in a town that was relatively small by Romano-British standards, shows just how rich the Church must have been in third-century Britain, and opens up a whole new chapter of understanding in the story of the Christian faith in these islands.

Christianity in Roman Britain is well-attested by archaeology and by documentary references. At the very end of the second century AD there was the country's first martyr, St Alban, who probably died during the persecutions of the emperor Caracalla at Verulamium (modern St Albans). In the fourth century, there were bishops recorded in Britain – some claimed they were too poor to attend the Council of Arles. It may have been as early as the second century that a cryptogram was scratched by a Christian on the wall of a house at Cirencester (Roman Corinium), though it is possible that the Christian significance of the graffito was not fully appreciated by the writer. It read:

ROTAS
OPERA
TENET
AREPO
SATOR

(Arepo the sower guides the wheels with work); if the letters are re-arranged they give PATER NOSTER, A and O – the first words of the Lord's Prayer and the first and last letters of the Greek alphabet, an allusion to 'I am the alpha and the omega, the beginning and the end' of the scriptures.

Romano-British churches are not well authenticated, but one was excavated at Silchester, in Hampshire, in the late nineteenth century, and re-excavated in 1961 by Professor Sir Ian Richmond. The church consisted of an apsed building, datable to around the middle of the fourth century AD. Certainly it did not enjoy a long life, for it had been abandoned and taken over by squatters in the 360s, as finds from the excavation proved. Orientated east–west, it consisted of a central portion, just over 29ft long and 10ft wide, flanked by two 5ft-wide side aisles with wider chambers or transepts at the west end, the northern one being cut off by a wall separating it from the north aisle. The apse was semi-circular, and contained a mosaic of abstract design. At the west end was a narthex or porch, in which the circular foundation perhaps took an offering-table for the unbaptised members of the congregation – a feature known from fifth-century churches in Syria. The western apse is a very rare feature in early churches, but is known at Cologne and in Rome. It has been suggested that this was a special kind of church known as a *memoria*, built in memory of a martyr whose body lay elsewhere. Outside the church a platform was found, with a tiled base and a soakaway, which was perhaps for ritual ablutions. Although it cannot be proved beyond doubt that the Silchester building is a church, all its features can be matched in other proven churches of the late Roman Empire and early post-Roman period, and it shows some which would be very remarkable in a pagan temple. On the strength of this, it seems likely that the Silchester building is the oldest church yet uncovered in Britain.

Of the same period as the Silchester church is the suite of Christian rooms in the Roman villa of Lullingstone, in Kent. Here, in the fourth century, what had formerly been a pagan shrine was converted to Christian use, to create a 'room shrine'. This recalled, no doubt intentionally, the 'upper room' where the Last Supper was

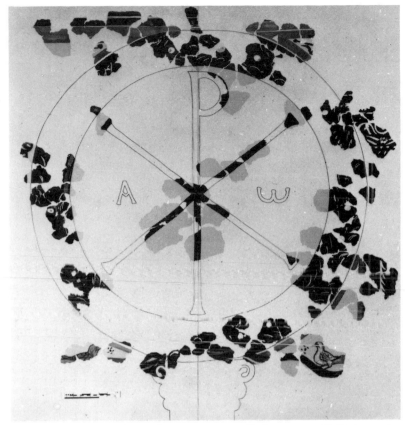

Example of a wall plaster from Lullingstone Roman Villa (*Department of the Environment*)

held, and is matched only at one other place in the empire – Dura
Europos, on the Euphrates. The later fourth-century occupants of the
Lullingstone villa seem to have used their home almost exclusively
for Christian worship, but they respected the old gods, and left the
statues of the 'ancestors' in a chamber below their room chapel. On
the chapel walls they painted a brightly coloured fresco depicting
praying figures in blue and saffron robes, edged with pearls, a curtain
draped behind them. Another fresco showed the Christogram in a
wreath, its fruits being pecked by doves.

The composite evidence suggests that, far from being an underground organisation, having to hide from authority and persecution, the Christians in Britain were flourishing openly in the centuries immediately following the birth of Christ.

The Followers of Odin

With the decline of Roman Britain, Christianity was kept alive in the old towns despite the rising tide of Anglo-Saxon invaders round their walls. It had always been strong in the west and north; now, away from the pagan menace of the Anglo-Saxons, it flourished in Wales and southern Scotland, to be nurtured into the Celtic Christian faith by newcomers from the Mediterranean. In the areas settled by the Anglo-Saxons, there is plenty of evidence for urban Christianity in the fifth and sixth centuries, and a peculiarly British heresy, Pelagianism, managed to take root in the fifth century. Some churches may have continued in use until the coming of St Augustine to convert the Anglo-Saxons. By tradition the church of St Martin, in Canterbury, was a Roman building used by Bertha, the Frankish queen of Kent, whose Christian chaplain may have been partly instrumental in preventing the Augustinian mission of 597.

There is surprisingly little archaeological evidence of the religion of the pagan Anglo-Saxons; though their deities are well known, no certain Saxon temple has ever been excavated. This may be because the Saxons, once converted, adapted their old temples into Christian churches. Several Anglo-Saxon deities gave their names to days of the week: Tiw, Tuesday; Woden, or Odin, Wednesday; Thor, Thursday, and Frig, Friday. Woden, the most important of the gods, was worshipped at Wednesbury and Wednesfield, and gave his name to the great linear earthwork of the Dark Ages known as Wansdyke. Tiw, who was god of war, gave his name to Tuesley. Froyle, Frobury and Frydaythorpe are named after Frig, goddess of love and mother of both men and gods. A number of festivals owe their origins to the pagan Saxons: Easter, despite being a Christian feast, is named after the Anglo-Saxon god, Eostre. Lammastide (1 August) comes from the Saxon *hlafmasse*, a time when loaves (*hlaf* is a loaf) were made from the first corn, as a thanks offering.

The fact that so little is known about them and their worship, makes the Anglo-Saxon gods more mysterious.

9

Riddles of the Stones

About 200 years ago a visitor to the hills near Callender in Tayside on May Day's eve would have been able to witness a remarkable pagan ceremony whose roots were deeply embedded in prehistory. The local people used to cut a circle in the turf, large enough for all those taking part to stand inside. Then a bonfire was lit. An oatcake would be broken into pieces – one of which was rubbed with charcoal – and placed in a bag. Each blindfolded participant took a piece out of the bag; the one who drew the blackened morsel was symbolically sacrificed to appease the elements and perpetuate the crops.

Such rituals are believed to go back beyond prehistoric times to the beginnings of farming itself in Britain. Stone Age and Bronze Age agriculturalists and pastoralists carried out similar rituals on the sites of the prehistoric stone and earth circles which have succeeded in baffling generations of antiquaries, archaeologists and folklorists. What is to be made of the circles of standing stones, often high up on desolate moors? Now they keep company with peewits and whinchats, but their weather-beaten and lichened faces bear silent testimony to the people who once gathered around them, perhaps to perform ceremonies which to modern minds would be both violent and obscene. Were these sites connected with some ancient knowledge of astronomy and mathematics, as some experts believe, or were they simply meeting places where axes could be traded and festivals celebrated amid singing and dancing?

Not only circles of standing stones – there are about 900 of them in

Ring of Brodgar, Orkney

Britain and Ireland — but countless single standing stones and alignments have survived from the same remote period. There are stones too with strange carvings, so painstakingly executed that they must have had some great importance for their carvers. If their code could only be cracked, it might open up a new chapter in understanding of the development of mankind.

Of all the natural substances used by man, none has proved as lasting and few as versatile as stone. From stone, ancient man fashioned the tools on which he relied for his very existence. In time, he learned to pile stone on stone to erect shelters for himself and his family, to make walls to pen his animals and protect them from marauders, to

The Hill o Many Stanes, Caithness. Prehistoric stone alignments.

build temples in which to worship his gods, and tombs in which to bury his dead. Timber and turf could be used for these purposes, but both lacked durability. Stone was eternal; it held out the promise that something involved in human endeavour could survive the transience of life itself. Stone thus answered one of the great needs of mankind – that of leaving behind something that will live on.

Its surface could be cut and ground, carved and abraded with patterns and symbols, images and signs. It could be decorated to satisfy artistic leanings; it could carry statements that would have no such permanence on wood or cloth. Stone had its uses not only for constructing the shrines and temples of the gods but for chronicling the very elements of ancient faith.

Rudston Monolith, Humberside (*Janet & Colin Bord*)

Stone monuments of past ages have attracted round them layer after layer of legend, mystery and history. Almost every parish in Britain has at least one stone with a story attached to it – it might be a slab carved with some ancient inscription, or a huge, natural boulder, quite unornamented by human hand, erected by long-dead people for some long-forgotten purpose. The strength of tradition is often so great that the sanctity of ancient stones is preserved, and folklore ensures that the mystery surrounding them is perpetuated from generation to generation.

Even Christianity has not been able to rob these relics of their prominence in local superstition. The tallest single standing stone in the British Isles still juts skyward in the churchyard at Rudston, in Yorkshire, while a circle of standing stones can be seen within the churchyard at Midmar, in Grampian. In 1560 the Synod of Argyll ordered the destruction of a stone circle on the holy island of Iona, because people still worshipped at it and because under its twelve stones men were said to have been 'buried alive'. In modern lore, standing stones play a part in witchcraft: in 1949 the Rollright Stones in Oxfordshire witnessed a May Sabat of witches. At Soussons Common, Devon, a lock of modern hair was unearthed in the stone cist in the centre of a circle of standing stones. Even today, the sovereigns of England are seated above an ancient block of meteoric stone, the Stone of Destiny, to be crowned in the full ceremonial of Christian belief.

Dunadd – Footprints in the Stone

Deep in the Western Highlands, dwarfed by the surrounding peaks, the craggy outcrop of Dunadd thrusts itself up from the flat fields of a valley. Despite the farm buildings at its base, Dunadd is a lonely place, full of menace. This is hardly surprising, for this hill fort witnessed some violent chapters in early Scottish history. It was the capital of the Scots – immigrants who crossed from Ireland in the fifth century AD. They created a kingdom for themselves in western Scotland and waged incessant war on the neighbouring Picts. In days

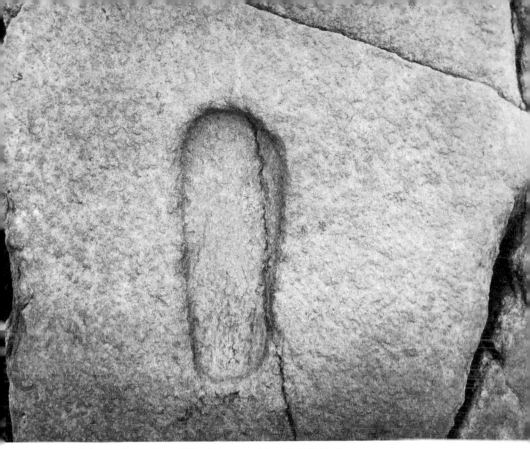

Carving of a human foot at Dunadd Dark Age Fort (*Janet & Colin Bord*)

gone by the now green fields were part of a great bog known as the Crinan Moss, and the twin rocky peaks of Dunadd, with its stone walls, became the hill fort of the kings of the Scots.

The three sets of carvings to be seen at Dunadd probably belong to the Dark Ages — sometime between the fifth century AD and the coming of the Vikings in the ninth. The first consists of two depressions in the rock face near the summit of the hill, deliberately cut to represent footprints. Though unusual, such foot marks are not unique. A very similar pair is carved on a boulder, known as the Ladykirk Stone, now in St Mary's Church, Burwick, on South

Roughting Linn inscribed stone, Northumberland (*Janet & Colin Bord*)

Ronaldsay in Orkney. Local tradition says that St Magnus, the patron saint of Orkney, sailed over the Pentland Firth on the stone and that these are his footprints. There is a stone similarly marked at the Iron Age fort at Clickhimin, in Shetland (see p 73), and others, referred to in documents, once existed in Ireland.

The explanation advanced for these foot carvings is that they were cut into inauguration stones – when a king was being crowned he stood with his feet in the prints. In Ireland, ceremonies where the chief-to-be stood on such a stone were carried out as late as the sixteenth century. Shoes are associated with inaugurations in many periods and countries, including ancient Greece.

The other carvings at Dunadd are even more mysterious. One is of a boar – if this was some kind of totem among the early Scots, why are there no similar representations in Ireland or elsewhere in Scottish territory? The carving is akin to the type of engravings done by the Picts, the neighbours and sworn enemies of the Scots, who are known to have had totemic symbols which included a boar. Could they have been executed by some victorious Pictish army, as a gesture of defiance which remained to shame the Scots after they had regained possession of their citadel?

It seems likely that the third carving was certainly produced by Picts, not Scots. This is an inscription in a mysterious script known as ogham. It cannot be deciphered, for the language of the Picts is lost and none of the ogham inscriptions from Pictish lands has ever been properly decoded. The key can be found not in Scotland but in Wales and Cornwall.

Vortepor's Tombstone

Among the stones housed in Carmarthen Museum, one is of exceptional interest. On its face it carries a Latin inscription:

MEMORIA

VOTEPORIGIS

PROTECTORIS

with a cross above. This is written in the kind of letters that were in use in Britain in the fifth and sixth centuries, after the Romans left. Translated, it means 'To the Memory of Vortepor, Protector'. Who was this Vortepor?

The tombstone was found at Castell Dwyran in Dyfed. Only important personages were commemorated by such tombstones, and on this rare occasion in Dark Age history the man concerned can be't identified. He is mentioned by Gildas, the sixth-century monk, who wrote an attack on some of his contemporaries, and also an account of the end of Roman Britain and the coming of the Anglo-Saxons. Gildas refers to a 'Vortepor, the stupid king and tyrant of Dyfed'. The date of Gildas' Vortepor (*c* AD 540–50) would approximate with that of the stone, and it is unlikely that two important people of the same name would be found at the same time in this part of Wales.

But what about 'Protector'? The title is a Roman one, though here it seems to have been a family name. In Roman times it was bestowed on officer-cadets in the army, and it may well have been that one of Vortepor's family had been so honoured long before, when Britain was still a part of the Roman Empire. Can the title be taken as evidence for a surviving respect for Roman institutions nearly a century and a half after the withdrawal of Roman troops from Britain?

The word 'Memoria' is also puzzling, for it was not usual in sixth-century Britain, but is found instead in North Africa and sometimes in Italy. Does its use indicate contact between these far-off lands and Wales in the time of Vortepor?

Ogham – the Secret Alphabet

Vortepor's tombstone poses another riddle. Down the side are cut a number of ogham signs, consisting of vertical strokes on a horizontal line. This primitive alphabet was developed in Ireland, but archaeologists have been unable to discover when and how or exactly where it originated. It is first encountered on similar tombstones in the fifth and sixth centuries, but probably evolved centuries previously. The characters are very like the cuts made on tally sticks, and from this it has been deduced that the alphabet evolved from tallies cut on pieces of wood, which have not survived. Ogham is found in Ireland and in areas in which the Irish settled in Western Britain. Most of the examples – many of them also carrying Latin inscriptions – have been located in Pembroke and adjacent parts of South Wales, in Cornwall and the Isle of Man. The presence of ogham on the tombstone of

Vortepor might suggest that he had Irish connections, but the inscription in Latin seems to contradict this possibility.

The Pictish Symbols

The Picts who acquired the ogham alphabet from their enemies, the Scots, are probably the most puzzling and mysterious of all the inhabitants of Britain in early historic times. An Icelandic writer of the thirteenth century described them thus:

> The Picts were little more than pygmies in height, working wonderfully in the mornings and evenings at building their towns but at noon losing all their strength and out of pure terror hiding themselves in underground dwellings. The [Orkney] islands were not called Orkneys but the land of the Picts, for which reason to this day the sea which separates the islands from Scotland is called the Pentland Firth.

Pict means 'painted man' – the name the Romans gave the Picts when they first appear in history in the third and fourth centuries AD, as one of the barbarian peoples who frequently raided Roman Britain. They were the native inhabitants of Scotland north of the Forth–Clyde line; though originally they may have occupied only the north-east region, by the time of their wars with the Scots their control extended throughout northern Scotland, including the Northern Isles.

In spite of their importance, which is attested by occasional mentions in the writings of outsiders, hardly anything is known about them. The Pictish language is lost, though some names of kings, place-names and a few words inscribed on stone and metal have survived. From such slender clues it has been deduced that the Picts were the native prehistoric peoples of Scotland, who had kept alive something of their pre-Celtic Bronze Age language down into historical times.

Although few traces of their homes and churches have ever come

129

to light, the Picts have left one important but puzzling group of relics. These consist of a very large number of inscribed stones and sculptures, ornamented with mysterious signs that have totally resisted repeated attempts to interpret them over the last two centuries.

The Pictish symbol stones fall into two categories. First there are crude undressed slabs and boulders, on which are incised a variety of signs. These are of two types: naturalistic representations of animals, most of which are real, not mythological; and abstract but often complex patterns usually referred to descriptively as, for example, 'notched rectangle and Z rod', 'crescent and V rod' and 'triple disc'. In the second category, the Picts later carved their symbols in relief on Christian grave slabs, combining the designs with crosses and Bible scenes. These disappear with the Picts themselves when the Scots overcame them in the ninth century.

Some deductions can be made about these symbols. Firstly, they were clearly not distasteful to the Christian Picts and therefore cannot be directly connected with any pagan cult. Secondly, they are uniform throughout Pictland, implying that they have actual meanings and are not simply subjects of artistic expression. Thirdly, they appear in particular combinations – symbols of animals with one or more abstract symbols.

The simplest explanation is that the symbols are clan and personal badges, rather like the coats-of-arms of later medieval times, used to denote the status of the deceased on tombstones or to mark out territorial boundaries. Their origin is equally mysterious. Some think they belong to an Iron Age past and depict Iron Age objects; others believe they were the invention of one great Pictish master-mind early in the Dark Ages, perhaps in the fifth century. While none appear to have been carved on stone before that date, they could have been executed in tattoo form.

Folklore has provided some explanation for the mysterious symbols. The Maiden Stone – one of the finest examples – which stands

Pictish stone at Aberlemno, Angus

by a roadside in a stretch of moorland at Chapel of Garioch, Grampian, is said to be the petrified body of Janet of Drumdurno, a girl who fell prey to the attempted seduction of a warlock. As she fled from his unwelcome advances, she burnt her apron with a hot breadshovel which according to the story accounts for the strange markings on the stone.

The Auld Wives' Lifts

Some 7 miles north of the centre of Glasgow, on Craigmaddie Muir, there is a huge block of sandstone supported by two others. The space beneath the capstone is narrow, and legend has it that anyone visiting the place for the first time must attempt to crawl through it or they will die childless. The group of stones is known locally as the 'Auld Wives' Lifts'; traditionally three old women, having made a bet as to who could carry the greatest burden, brought the three stones to the site in their aprons.

Scientific explanations as to how these boulders reached their present positions are inconclusive. For various reasons, the suggestion that they are glacial erratics has not found favour with geologists, while archaeologists are not happy with the idea of them having been erected by the hand of man. Nineteenth-century antiquaries believed the Lifts to be the remains of a Druid altar, and spoke of the 'gruesome but not altogether disagreeable feeling pervading us as we stand upon the stone of blood'. Not until 1975 did anyone detect that the stones had been carved in antiquity. Professor Leslie Alcock – the excavator of the supposed site of Camelot (see p 78) – visited the site in varying lighting conditions and produced photographs of a series of heads carved on the Lifts. Earlier photographs, taken in Victorian times, show at least one of the heads clearly. Yet, despite the fascination of these Lifts for antiquaries, the carvings were simply not noticed – like those on the stones of Stonehenge (see p 139) that escaped detection until the 1950s.

A key to the Lift carvings is provided by one of the heads, which is adorned with horns – a style of representation that at once recalls ancient Iron Age carvings of the Celtic god Cernunos. From the similar style of the other carvings it seems very likely that the Lifts were carved in the Iron Age, perhaps around the first century AD, by the followers of the Druids. Thus, some of the nineteenth-century antiquaries' guesses that the Lifts had Druidical connections may not be so very far from the truth.

Why carve such heads? From all over Britain similar carvings have come to light. Most were executed in three-dimensional relief; some are faintly comical, while others are frankly frightening. That some at least date back to the Iron Age can be proved by the fact that they have turned up on Roman sites in contexts datable to the first and second centuries AD, and from the fact that similar heads appear sometimes in Iron Age Celtic art. Not all are as ancient; a series found in Yorkshire includes carvings of traditional design which have been executed in the twentieth century. It seems astonishing that such a tradition of carving heads should be kept alive in England for over 2,000 years, but experts believe this is quite possible.

In the recent past such heads were regarded as lucky, and were built into the walls of buildings to provide protection. In the Iron Age world of the Celts the stone heads had a much more sinister connection. They represent artistic evidence of the practice of head-hunting, and for the veneration of the head as the seat of the pagan Celtic equivalent of the soul. Archaeologists, digging on the site of an Iron Age fort at Breedon, discovered that severed heads had adorned the gateway – tangible proof of this head cult.

The ancient Celtic cult had been kept alive for centuries on the island of Vatersay in the Hebrides, as a modern Scots Gaelic folk tale demonstrates. It narrates how three brothers were murdered at the 'Well of the Heads'. Their father found the bodies and then beheaded them. He took the heads past an ancient standing stone; at once one head came to life and announced that the living man, of whom it had been part, had made a girl pregnant and that, when the child grew up, it would avenge the death of its uncles. The story not only

Bryn Celli Ddu burial chamber in Anglesey showing the carved stone at the back
(*Janet & Colin Bord*)

embodies a severed head element but also something of the Celtic veneration of water.

The Great 'Eye Goddess'

Deeply carved on some of the stones of the prehistoric chambered tombs of Britain and Ireland (see p 20) are mysterious designs. The most elaborate of these appear on the tombs of the Boyne Valley in Ireland, such as New Grange, Dowth and Knowth, but they are also pecked into the stones of tombs in Scotland and North Wales.

There are some fine carvings to be seen in the tombs at Bryn Celli Ddu and Barclodiad y Gawres in Gwynedd. The Bryn Celli Ddu carving consists of a spiral cut on a stone in the central chamber, and a more ornate design on a slab which had been buried in a pit before the mound was constructed – and was therefore quite invisible when the tomb was in use. Most of the designs are abstract: zigzags, triangles, lozenges, spirals, circles, rayed circles, crosses and scallops. Some, much less impersonal, represent pairs of eyes, sometimes with brows added and even noses. This 'face' – the 'eye goddess', as it is called – is not confined to the walls of chambered tombs in Britain and Ireland, but is also found elsewhere – most of these designs can be matched in Spain for instance. A very good example adorns a pillar at Gavr'innis in Britanny, where there is also a carving of a flat bronze or copper axe, which seems to have been cut into the stone long before such a tool was in general use in the region.

There can be little doubt that these carvings have a religious meaning. Some seem to have been carved with great care and afterwards concealed from human eyes, as at Bryn Celli Ddu. This was also the case at New Grange in Ireland, where the backs of several stones lining the passage were decorated – though it is possible that these were rough sketches done by the artist before executing the finished design on the faces of other stones.

When, earlier this century, archaeologists believed that the chambered tombs all originated in one place and spread outwards through

Europe, the 'eye' carvings could be easily explained as being part of the trappings of a cult of some goddess, perhaps a great earth mother. But the tombs are now known to have developed independently in various regions, and the 'eye goddess' must be considered as perhaps a symbol of a curious prehistoric religion whose practitioners sometimes built chambered tombs.

The 'eye goddess' also appears as a decoration on pots in Scandinavia, Spain, Germany and France, and on three chalk drums or 'idols' found in a child's grave at Folkton, in Yorkshire. Similar eyes adorn some mysterious carved stone balls from Scotland, which are found particularly commonly in Aberdeenshire. These are carefully fashioned, but archaeologists cannot even guess at their function. Were they used in some religious ritual, in a game, or as the weights for *bolas* – a kind of sling used for hunting? Perhaps it was felt that to adorn *bolas* weights with the symbol of the eye goddess would render them more effective in bringing down their prey?

These carved stone balls were shown to belong to the period of the chambered tombs following excavations at one of Britain's most prehistoric sites – Skara Brae, in Orkney.

The 'Writing' on the Walls of Skara Brae

This village is known to have been occupied around 2000 BC by Stone Age fishermen and farmers, who were contemporaries of the tomb builders. Here a carved stone ball was found, with other mysterious carvings on the walls and adorning some pots.

When Skara Brae was engulfed by a sandstorm, all the houses survived intact, except for their roofs. Inside, the furniture was discovered still in position – for, in the absence of timber in Orkney, the dressers, beds and other items were constructed of stone slabs. On one dresser were the remains of a crushed pot abandoned in antiquity. The inhabitants of this prehistoric British 'Pompeii' lived in a semi-subterranean warren; the entire village being covered by a midden to keep out the cold Atlantic winds and the driving rain of winter.

Engravings still to be seen on the walls of the passages of Skara Brae look like some form of writing, but include patterns reminiscent of those found in chambered tombs.

The ubiquitous 'eye goddess' is carved on a stone in a tomb on the island of the Holm of Papa Westray, in the Orkneys, which may have been built by contemporaries of the Skara Brae people. Are these designs purely abstract or some kind of primitive pictographic script? Writing is generally believed to have developed in the Near East around 3000 BC, but did not reach Europe for over a thousand years, by which time Skara Brae had long since become a mound of sand. However, script-like signs have been discovered on tablets at a site called La Tartaria, in Romania, which are at least as old as any

Example of cup-and-ring marks (*Department of the Environment*)

unearthed in the Near East. The use of various symbol 'pictograms' to represent ideas could have been developed in many areas independently, and it is not inconceivable that people as advanced in other ways as the Stone Age and Bronze Age inhabitants of Britain had initiated some kind of sign writing – albeit more primitive than an alphabet – as early as 2000 BC.

The Cup-and-Ring Marks

If any symbols can be said to approach a form of sign writing in prehistoric Britain the most likely contenders are the cup-and-ring marks of the Bronze Age, so-called because the most characteristic consists of a hollow or 'cup' pecked into the surface of a stone, often surrounded by one or more circles or 'rings'. These carvings are to be seen on rock faces all over the highland regions. So many of them have come to light that a full inventory has never been made, but it is quite clear that they were executed during the course of a very long period. One of the earliest was found beneath the mound of a Stone Age tomb dated to around 3240 BC; other examples appear on stones built into structures of the first or second century AD or even later – though these could have been introduced when old stones were reused for the building.

The most interesting group of such carvings appears on the stones of Bronze Age burial mounds. Alongside the cup-and-ring marks are other engravings – some obviously related to the earlier designs found on Stone Age chambered tombs, such as spirals and lozenges; there are others, too, such as hand-and-axe signs, which do not occur in earlier times.

The designs of the cup-and-ring marked stones are not peculiar to Britain; but, curiously, similar occurrences on the Continent are of a later date. This has led to the suggestion that it is some kind of native British art which may have spread to Spain and elsewhere through overseas trade.

But what do these cup-and-ring marks mean? It is quite clear that they are not random scribblings; one expert, Professor Thom, has shown that in diameter they measure multiples of a unit which he calls a 'megalithic inch'. One suggestion is that they are solar symbols, perhaps connected with the same kind of sky cult sometimes associated with stone circles. The axes frequently found near stone circles in Britain may have had something to do with the cult, which would explain why the symbol of an axe is carved on some of the cup-and-ring marked stones. Carvings of hands, and the occasional foot, may be marks of divinity or of regal status – as with the footprints at Dunadd – though in other societies such symbols have been associated with death. Most interpretations of the cup-and-ring marks imply some religious connotation, but it has also been pointed out that they could have a more mundane meaning – perhaps serving as prospectors' signs to mark a likely location of copper or good stone.

Stonehenge

Stonehenge has always been famous and mysterious. In the Middle Ages monks drew impressions of it, and related how it had been put up by the magic of the wizard Merlin. In the sixteenth century the antiquary William Camden wrote:

About sixteen miles northward of Salisbury, on the Plains is to be seen *insana substructio*, a wild structure. For within a trench are plac'd huge unhewn stones in 3 circles, oen within the other, in the manner of a Crown, some of which are 28 foot in height, and seven in breadth, on which others like *Architraves* are born up, so that it seems to be a hanging pile; from whence we call it Stonehenge, as the ancient Historians from its greatness call'd it *Gigantum Chorea*, the Giants dance . . . Our country-men reckon this among the wonders of the land. For it is unaccountable how such stones should come there, seeing all the circumjacent country want ordinary stones for building; and also by what means they were raised . . . Yet it is the opinion of some, that these stones are not

Stonehenge (*Aldus Books*)

natural or such as are dug out of the rock but artificial, being made
of fine sand concreted together by a glewy sort of matter.

Each age in turn has asked the same questions about Stonehenge:
Who built it? Why? How was it put up? And in each age the answers
are different, according to the views of the time.

Some progress has been made on the subject of Stonehenge since
Camden's day. We now know that the temple was built long before the
time of the Celtic Druids who for so long were believed to have been
its builders. Indeed, the 'Druid Temple' explanation of Stonehenge
dies a slow death. In the early morning of 23 June – Midsummer's Eve
– members of the Church of the Druid Universal Bond perform their
rites in honour of the summer solstice. A fine panoply of costumed
figures in scarlet hoods, with the Archdruid in his white robes and
imitation Bronze Age Irish necklet, wait through the night for the
sun to rise and shed its first light on the Altar Stone. Although this is a
modern ceremony, and these Druids are in fact a recent creation out of

eighteenth-century whimsy, it nevertheless embodies the reverence and interest that has been shown in the monument through the ages.

The beginnings of Stonehenge go back to around 3000 BC or a little later, when Early Neolithic farmers dug out the ditch that surrounds it to form a ritual enclosure; round this they dug a series of ritual pits – known as the Aubrey holes after their famous seventeenth-century discoverer, John Aubrey. Apart from these pits, Stonehenge was little different from other ritual enclosures in Britain at the time, for as yet the only stones to be put up were the two portals – the Slaughter Stone and Heel Stone.

The next chapter in Stonehenge's history opens with the erection of a double circle of 'bluestones', but the designers changed their minds before this was completed and decided on a new layout – a processional way, now called the Avenue, marked by standing stones from the banks of the Avon. There was nothing unusual about building a circle of standing stones, but the bluestone circle at Stonehenge was rather different from most of its contemporaries. For one thing, the stones with which it was constructed had come from the Presceli Mountains of South Wales; whether they had been found as glacial erratics, which is most unlikely, or had been transported all the way from Presceli, which is probable, no other surviving stone circle in the British Isles was built with stones from so distant a source. Geoffrey of Monmouth, writing in the Middle Ages, was quite categorical that the bluestones came from Mount Killaurus in Ireland; while this is certainly not the case, it may preserve a genuine folk tradition that the stones were not local but transported from far-off lands. This phase of Stonehenge has been dated to around 2150 BC; it is clear from the way the new builders began to dig a circle round the Heel Stone and then filled it in again with chalk that the old traditions were still venerated.

One fact is seemingly indisputable about the first two phases of construction at Stonehenge: both were concerned with maintaining the alignments of the stones, which were determined by the midsummer and midwinter sun positions.

Why was this second phase of building abandoned before the bluestone circles had been completed? Almost certainly it was because a new, exciting period in the history of prehistoric Wessex was opening up. Eclipsed in size by such neighbouring giant circles as Avebury, if not in the effort involved in transporting the stones, the Stonehenge builders decided to go one better. Copper technology had come to Wessex; the chiefs were growing rich, furnishing their graves with gold and rare amber from the northern lands. Some of these chiefs, if not all, were merchant princes from foreign shores, who knew the kind of power wealth could bring. Prehistorians disagree about the nature of these copper lords and whether they were as wealthy as their burials seem to suggest; they also dispute whether these chiefs of the Wessex Culture, as it is called, were responsible for building Stonehenge III – as we see it today – or whether it was put up by the natives at the time of their arrival, c 1800 BC.

Whoever planned it, they excelled. And what a labour it was! It required the back-breaking efforts of hundreds, even thousands, for many, many years. No fewer than seventy-seven giant sarsens, each averaging 26 tons, were dragged from the Marlborough Downs. It has been reckoned it would have taken two months to drag one such stone to the site, even with a workforce of a thousand or more. They may have transported only one stone a year.

Once on the site, the stones were pounded into shape with stone mauls, rubbed smooth, then hoisted up. The unique 40-ton lintels had sockets carefully cut in them to receive the pegs of a tenon-and-mortice joint. The outcome was a perfect circle composed of thirty stones with thirty lintels, inside which was set a horseshoe of five trilithons open to the north-east. So as not to waste the rare bluestones, at a later stage these were re-erected; the plan was to set them in a spiral, but this was never completed. The stones ended up in their present positions – sixty round the trilithons, nineteen in a horseshoe within them. In the centre was the Altar Stone, alone and magnificent.

The axis of the monument was altered slightly – perhaps because of the slight change in the midsummer sunrise over the centuries, perhaps because the builders were now more interested in the midwinter sunset.

Speculation about the exact nature of Stonehenge is as rife today as it ever was. Some see it as a giant computer; some as some kind of observatory, and others as simply a religious monument connected with the farming calendar. Whatever its function, it certainly played an important role in the religion of Bronze Age man in Wessex, a role which is forever lost to us.

APPENDIX I

Where To See Britain's Mysterious Sites

1 – Secrets of the Grave

Although many of the burial places mentioned in chapter I cannot now be visited or, if they can, offer nothing for the visitor to see, there are hundreds of other prehistoric chambered tombs and unchambered burial mounds in all parts of Britain, and almost without exception they are fascinating and mysterious places. The following selection includes two spectacular attractions – Silbury Hill and Maes Howe.

Silbury Hill, Wilts (SU 100685). About 6 miles W of Marlborough, the mound can be seen to the S of the A4, less than 1 mile due S of Avebury.

Maes Howe, Mainland, Orkney (HY 318128). About 9 miles W of Kirkwall, on the A965.

West Kennet Long Barrow, Avebury, Wilts (SU 104677). A classic example of a megalithic chambered tomb, not far from Silbury Hill, just to the S of the A4.

Wayland's Smithy, Uffington, Oxfordshire (SU 281854). Another classic chambered tomb, less than a mile S of the B4507, about 8 miles W of Wantage.

Kit's Coty House, nr Aylesford, Kent (TQ 745608). Now denuded of its mound, the stones of this tomb are still very impressive. On a side road, just W of the A229, about 1 mile N of Aylesford.

2 – Royal Mysteries and Murders

Tower of London, in City of London, on Tower Hill.

Berkeley Castle, Glos (ST 6899). At Berkeley, just E of the B4509, reached from the M5 and A38.

Corfe Castle, Dorset (SY 9681). On the A351, about 5 miles SE of Wareham.

Holyrood Palace, Edinburgh, Lothian. At the foot of the Canongate, Edinburgh.

3 – Giants in Chalk

Wandlebury, and *Gog Magog Hills,* Cambs (TL 494534). About 4 miles SE of Cambridge, on the A604.

Cerne Giant, Dorset (ST 666016). At Cerne Abbas, about 7 miles N of Dorchester on the A352, on the hillside to the E of the road.

Long Man of Wilmington, East Sussex (TQ 543035). Near Wilmington village S of the A27, about 5 miles NW of Eastbourne.

Uffington White Horse, Oxfordshire (SU 299863). Although not strictly speaking a 'giant', this is one of the finest and oldest chalk-out 'white horses' in England. Adjacent to an Iron Age hillfort, it can be reached by a side road due S of the B4507, about 7 miles W of Wantage.

4 – Heroes and Myths from Britain's History

Glastonbury, Somerset (ST 5039). On the junction of the A39, A361 and B3151, about 22 miles NE of Taunton. There are a number of sites with Arthurian associations in Glastonbury: the Abbey where King Arthur was supposedly buried; Glastonbury Tor, which excavation has shown to have been occupied in the time of Arthur, and the Chalice Well, at the foot of the Tor, where the Holy Grail was said to be hidden.

Tintagel, Cornwall (SX 049891). Tintagel Castle, reputedly the birthplace of Arthur, can be approached from the village of Tintagel on the B3263, about 4 miles SW of Boscastle. Merlin's cave can be seen by following the path beneath the castle rock.

Liddington Castle, Wiltshire (SU 2079). Iron Age hillfort, occupied at the time of Arthur, and the possible site of the battle of Mons Badonicus. Reached from Liddington, on the A419, about 4 miles S of Swindon at junction 15 of the M4.

Badbury Rings, Dorset (ST 964030). Another Iron Age fort, contender for

Mons Badonicus. Just N of the B3082, nearly 6 miles SE of Blandford Forum.

Winchester, Hants (SU 4829). 10 miles N of Southampton. The medieval King Arthur's round table is here.

St Michael's Mount, Cornwall (SW 5130). At Marazion, on the A394.

Roslin, Lothian (NT 2763). Reached by minor roads from the A703, about 1½ miles s of Loanhead, about 8 miles s of Edinburgh.

5 – Castles and Citadels

Broch of Mousa, Shetland (HU 457237). On the W shore of Mousa island, facing the mainland; reached by boat from Sandwick.

Midhowe, Rousay, Orkney (HY 371308). On the shore on the W of Rousay island; reached by the B9064 and thence across rough ground.

Broch of Gurness, Mainland, Orkney (HY 383268). About 11 miles NW of Kirkwall, on the A966; then by footpath for about 1½ miles.

Clickhimin, Mainland, Shetland (HU 464408). On the outskirts of Lerwick; approached on foot from the A970.

Glenelg, Dun Telve and Dun Troddan, Inverness (NG 829172 and 834172). Reached by minor road off the A87 at Shiel Bridge, travelling 8 miles W.

Dun Carloway, Lewis (NB 190413). About 1½ miles SW of Carloway, 15 miles WNW of Stornoway off the A858.

St Andrews Castle, Fife (NO 513169). On the shore in St Andrews

Hereford Beacon, Great Malvern, Hereford & Worcester (SO 760400). Just s of the A449, 3 miles NE of Ledbury, 4 miles s of Great Malvern.

Glamis Castle, Tayside (NO 3846). Just E of the A928, about 3 miles s of Kirriemuir.

South Cadbury Castle, Somerset (ST 6325). 7 miles NE of Yeovil, reached by minor roads from the A359 or A303.

Richborough, Kent (TR 3260). 1½ miles NW of Sandwich. Reached by a minor road N off the A257 to Canterbury.

6 – Caves and Caverns

Cheddar Gorge, Somerset (ST 4654). On the A371, about 7 miles NW of Wells.

Wookey Hole, Mendips, Somerset (ST 531480). 1½ miles NW of Wells, reached by minor roads from the A371.

Kent's Cavern, Torquay, Devon (sx 930650). On the edge of Torquay, reached by the A379, and side road. Extensively quarried away.

Goat's Hole Cave, Paviland, West Glamorgan (ss 437859). About 15 miles w of Swansea. Access difficult because of tides. In the early nineteenth century Dean Buckland found the first Palaeolithic burial here. Reached by the A4118, B4247 and on foot thereafter.

Cresswell Crags, Derbyshire (sk 535742). Caves in the Derbyshire Peaks, occupied by Old Stone Age man. About 14 miles SE of Sheffield. Reached by the A616 and side road, to E.

St Ninian's Cave, Physgill, Wigtown (NX 422360). Reached by the A747, 3 miles sw of Whithorn and track to the s to Kidsdale Farm, then by a footpath.

St Molaise's Cave, Holy Island, Arran (NS 0529). On the w shore of the island; reached in summer by boat from Lamlash or Whiting Bay. The cave is less than a mile's walk from the pier.

7 – Hoaxes and Forgeries

Piltdown Skull, London. The British Museum, Department of Natural History, Cromwell Rd.

Other examples of forged work can be seen at the British Museum in Bloomsbury.

8 – Lost Gods, Their Supporters and Adversaries

Temple of Mithras, Walbrook, London; re-erected outside Temple Court, 11 Victoria St, 60 yards or so from its original site.

Temple of Mithras, Carrawburgh, Northumberland (NY 8571). At the Roman fort of Brocolitia, on Hadrian's Wall. Reached by the B6318, about 10 miles NW of Hexham.

Lullingstone, Kent (TQ 5365). Reached by a side road off the A225 in Eynsford.

9 – Riddles of the Stones

Dunadd, Strathclyde (NR 8393). 1½ miles w of Kilmichael Glassary, 4 miles NW of Lochgilphead, off the A816; approached by a farm road to the w.

Vortepor's Tombstone, Dyfed (SN 4120). In Carmarthen Museum, Quay St.

Maiden Stone, Grampian (NJ 7024). On a side road NW off the A96 about 6 miles NW of Inverurie, S from Mill of Carden to Chapel of Garioch.

Aberlemno, Tayside (NO 5255). 5 miles NE of Forfar. Two fine Pictish symbol stones in an enclosure to the S of the B9134; another stone in the old churchyard, reached by a side road to the S.

St Vigean's, Tayside (NO 6342). One of the two finest collections of Pictish stones, 1½ miles N of Arbroath on a minor road.

Meigle, Tayside (NN 2844). The other fine collection of Pictish stones, 6 miles NE of Coupar Angus on the A94 to Forfar.

The Auld Wives' Lifts, Strathclyde (NS 582764). On Craigmaddie Muir, reached by the A81, about 10 miles N of Glasgow.

Bryn Celli Ddu, Gwynedd (SH 5070). Reached by the A4080 and a side road N, about 4 miles SW of Menai Bridge.

Skara Brae, Mainland, Orkney (HY 231188). On the Bay of Skaill, about 6 miles NNW of Stromness, along the B9056.

Stonehenge, Wilts (SU 123422). On the A344, 2 miles W of Amesbury.

Ring of Brodgar, Mainland, Orkney (HY 294134). With the adjacent *Stenness Stones*, forms part of a complex centring on the Lochs of Harray and Stenness, on the B9055.

Chronology of Events

Prehistory to Modern Times

Palaeolithic
*c*250000–*c*7500 BC

Old Stone Age, divided into Lower, Middle and Upper Palaeolithic. First men in Britain in Lower Palaeolithic. Some caves occupied in Middle Palaeolithic by Neanderthal Man; main cave occupation in Upper Palaeolithic, period of last Great Ice Age, *c*12000–8300 BC.

Mesolithic
*c*7500–4000 BC or later

Middle Stone Age. Period when men still depended on hunting and fishing, but followed herds of game and lived in forests and coastal caves after retreat of the ice. Britain finally severed from Continent, *c*6000 BC.

Neolithic
*c*4000 (or earlier)–*c*2000 BC

New Stone Age. Period when food gathering was replaced by food production (farming). Pottery first used in Britain. Period of the Megalithic (ie 'big stone') chambered tombs and other collective burial mounds; and ritual enclosures, including early 'henges' and 'causewayed camps'. Skara Brae occupied at end of period.

Beaker Period
*c*2400–2000 BC

Term used by archaeologists to describe very end of Neolithic when copper was first being used but bronze not developed. Collective burial in megalithic tombs ousted by single burials under round mounds (barrows). Some more elaborate henges and stone circles (eg Avebury) erected.

Bronze Age
*c*2000–700 BC

Bronze in widespread use for edge tools. Many stone circles and single standing stones erected. Stonehenge belongs to this period. Period of heroic warrior society. Growth of trade.

Iron Age
*c*700 BC–AD 43

Iron working introduced from Continent and gradually replaced bronze for edge tools. Hillforts, which began in Middle Bronze Age, considerably developed. Celts dominant people in Britain. In late second century BC partly Celtic Belgae arrive in SE England. Introduce potter's wheel, coins and new types of fort. Fight with Julius Caesar, 55 and 54 BC, and with the forces of Claudius, AD 43.

The Roman Period
AD 43–450 or later

Conquest by Romans of most of southern Britain complete by late first century AD. Timber buildings in forts and towns replaced by stone in second century, when many mosaics laid down. No real civil occupation in Scotland, north and central Wales, the SW peninsula and England N of York – in these areas native Celtic peoples kept up many of their old ways.

The Dark Ages
c AD 400–1066

Roman army pulled out gradually in late fourth and early fifth century to deal with troubles elsewhere in Roman Empire. Roman life continued in towns through fifth century, when the Anglo-Saxons were settling in England. Celts continued to live in Scotland, Wales, SW peninsula and parts of N England, though Anglo-Saxons gradually penetrated and influenced most areas

except Scotland N of Forth–
Clyde line, and north Wales.
Late fifth and sixth centuries
the age of folk heroes, such as
King Arthur.

The Middle Ages
1066–1485

The period often taken as
beginning with the end of the
Roman occupation, but here
starting with the arrival of
William the Conqueror in
1066 and ending with the
defeat of Richard III by Henry
Tudor at Bosworth in 1485.

Modern Times
1485 to date

Royal Dynasties or Houses (1066 to date)

Normans	1066–1154	William I, William II, Henry I, Stephen
Plantagenets	1154–1399	Henry II, Richard I, John Henry III, Edward I, Edward II, Edward III, Richard II
Lancaster	1399–1461	Henry IV, Henry V, Henry VI
York	1461–85	Edward IV, Edward V, Richard III
Tudors	1485–1603	Henry VII, Henry VIII, Edward VI, Mary, Elizabeth I
Stuarts	1603–88	James I, Charles I, Charles II, James II
Commonwealth	1649–60	Cromwell (protector)
Orange	1689–1714	William and Mary, William III, Anne
Hanover	1714–1911	George I, II, III, IV, William IV, Victoria, Edward VII
Windsor	1911 to date	George V, Edward VIII, George VI, Elizabeth II

Index

Italics indicate illustrations

Aikerness, Orkney, 73
Ambrosius Aurelianus, 61
Amesbury Bank, Epping Forest, 62
Anastasius (Emperor), 27
Ancient Order of Purbeck Marblers, 36
Anglo-Saxon Chronicle, 52
Anglo-Saxon England, 27-8
Anglo-Saxons, 52, 60
antler picks, 14, 24
Arthur (King), 56-61, 78, 80
Auld Wives' Lifts, 132-5
Aulus Plautius, 77
Avebury Henge, 12

Badbury Rings, 56, 58
baldric mounts, 27
Ballareare, Isle of Man, 18
Bannockburn (battle), 34
barrows, 16
Bath, 12
Beaker period, 26
Beaton, Cardinal David, 76
Beauchamp Tower, 32
Bedd Branwen, 16
Benllech, 122
Berkeley Castle, 33-5, 34
blockhouse, 73
Bloody Tower, 32

Boadicea see Boudicca
Bothwell, Earl of, 41
Boudicca, Queen of Iceni, 13, 61-2, 62
Brenig Valley, 16
Broch of Mousa, 70, 75
brochs, 68-75
Bruce, Robert, 93
Bryn Celli Ddu, 134, 135
Buckingham, Duke of, 32
Bush Barrow, 65
Byzantine silver bowls, 27

Cadbury castle, 78-80, 79
Caerleon-upon-Usk, 56-7
Caernarvon castle, 33
Caesar, Julius, 25, 29, 108
Callender, 120
Camelot, 78-80
Canaanites, 63
cannibalism, 16-17
Caratacus, 76-8
Carausius, 83-6
Carn Liath Broch, 72
Carrawburgh, 111, mithraeum, 113, 114
Cartumandua, 78
Castell Dwyran, 127
castles, 67-86
caverns, 87-94

caves, 87-94
Celts, 42, 60, 66, 77, 89, 133
Cerne Abbas, 44
Cerne Giant, 44, *45*
Chalice Well, *53*, 54
chalk, 24, 42-7
Cheddar Gorge, 88
Christianity, 114-18
Christians, 27, 28
Cirencester, 115
citadels, 67-86
Clickhimin, 73
Clyde, 98-100
Cnut (King), 50
Colchester, 61
Constantius Chlorus, 85-6
Corfe castle, 35, 36-8, *37*
Coventry, 50
Craigmaddie Muir, 132
crannogs, 98-100
Crichel Down, 26
cup-and-ring marks, *137*, 138-9

Danebury Hants, 17
Danes, 52
Danish Raiders, 44
Darnley (Lord), 40-1
dogs, 25
Dozmary Pool, 56
Druids, 25, 108-9, 110
Dunadd, 73, 124-7, *125*
Dunbuie, 98, 99
Dun Carloway, 73, *75*
Dun Dornadilla, 73
Dunstan, 38
Dun Telve, 71, *74*
Dun Troddan, 71

earbones, 16-17
Edinshall, 75
Edward I, 32
Edward II, 33-5, 49
Edward IV, 32
Edward V, 32

Edward VII, 65
Edward the Martyr, 36-8
Egyptians, 64
Elizabeth I, 39
Ely, 52
Excalibur, 56
'Eye Goddess', 135-6

faience, 64
Finglesham, Kent, 47
firearms, 68
Flint Jack, 96-8
forgeries, 95-106
Fotheringay, 39
Francis II, K of France, 39

Galahad, Sir, 58
Geoffrey of Monmouth, 42, 57
giants, 42-7
Gildas, 128
Glamis, 80-2, *81*
Glastonbury, Somerset, 54
Glenelg Brock, *74*
Godda, 51
Godiva, Lady, 49-50
gods, 107-19
Gogmagog, 42-4
Gough's Cave, Cheddar, 88
graves, 11-28, 38
Greeks, 66
Greenhithe, Kent, 25
Guinevere, Queen, 56, 57, 58

Hamilton, Patrick, 76
Henry of Lancaster, 34
Hercules, 44
Hereford, 51
Hereford Beacon, 76, 77, *77*, 78
Hereward the Wake, 52
hermits, 90-3
heroes, 48-66
hoaxes, 95-106
Holy Grail, 52, 54-5, 58, 59
Holyrood Castle, Edinburgh, 40-1, *40*

Holy Thorn, 54
Holywell, Clwyd, 111
human sacrifice, 16-17

Iceni, tribe, 61
Iron Age, 25, 43
Isabella, Queen, 34-5

Jarlshof, Shetland, 73
Jesus, 54
John, King, 36, 38-9
Joseph of Arimethea, 52-3

King Sil, 12, 14
Kit's Coty House, 22
Kirklees Abbey (Park), 49
Knowes of Trotty, Orkney, 22

Lady Jane Grey, 32
Lancelot, Sir, 58
Langbank, 98-9
Late Stone Age, 21
Leofric, Earl of Mercia, 50
Lethbridge, T C, 43
Liddington Castle, 76
Little John, 49
Londinium, 61, 82
London, 12
Long Man of Wilmington, 44-7, 46
Lullingstone, 117, 117

Maes Howe, Orkney, 18-22, 18
Magna Carta, 38
Maiden Stone, 131-2
Maltravers, Sir John, 34
Mary, Queen of Scots, 39-41
'Master of the Gliding Gouge', 26
Megalithic chambered tombs, 42
Midhowe, Orkney, 71
Minster, Kent, 66
Mycenaeans, 65
Mithras, 112-14
Modred, 59
monasteries, 91

Mons Badonicus, battle of, 56, 59
More, Sir Thomas, 32-3
Mortimer, 34-5
Mousa, Shetland, 70, 71
murders, 29-41
myths, 48-66

Natural History Museum, London,
  102
Nennius, 59
Neolithic, 14, 26, 64
Newstead, Roman fort, 25
Normans, 51, 67
Normanton Gorse, Wilts, 22-4

Odin, 118-19
Offa's Dyke, 51
Ogham, 128-9
Orkney Isles, 69

Peeping Tom, 51
Pevensey, 104
Phoenicians, 62-3
Picts, 68
Pictish symbols, 129-32, 131
Piltdown Man, 100-4, 101
pottery, 23, 66
Prasutagus, King of the Iceni, 61
Prentice Pillar, 54-6, 55
psychometrists, 14

Raedwald, King of East Anglia, 28
rape, 18
Richard III (D of Gloucester), 32-3
Richard of Cirencester, 104-6
Richard the Lionheart, 32
Rillaton Cup, 65
Rillaton Manor, Cornwall, 65
Ring of Brodgar, 121
Rizzio, 41-4
Robert the Bruce, 34
Robin Hood, 48-9
Roger, John, 76
Rollright Stones, 124

Romans, 12, 60-2, 67, 78, 82-6
Rosslyn Chapel, Midlothian, 54
Roughting Linn, *126*
'Rough Wooing', 39
Rudstone Monolith, *123*

Sewerby, Humberside, 17
shaft, 22
Shetland Isles, *69*
ship, 28
shoulder clasps, 27
Silchester, 116
Silbury Hill, Wilts, 12-16, *13, 15*, 21
Skara Brae, Orkney, 136-8
skeletons, 17, 25
slave, 18
Snowdonia, 16
South Cadbury, Somerset, *60*, 61
spoons, 27
St Albans, 61
St Andrews Castle, 76
St Madron's Well, 111-12
St Michael's Mount, Cornwall, 63, *64*
  66
St Molaise' Cave, Arran, 92
St Ninian's Cave, Wigtown, 91-2, *92*
Stonehenge, 139-43, *140*
Stow, Lincs, 50
Stukeley, William, 104-6
Sutton Hoo, 27-8
Swanwick, Hants, 24
sword pommel, 27

Teignmouth, Devon, 66

television, 23
Tennyson, Lord, 59
Thomas, Lord of Berkeley Castle, 34
Tintagel Castle, *57*
Togodumnus, 77
tools, 14
Tower of London, 29, *30*
treasure, 38-9
trepanning, 25-6
Turold, Abbot of Peterborough, 52
Twyne, John, 63

urn, 16

Vikings, 18, 20
Vortepor, 127-8

Wallace, William, 93-4
Wandlebury, Cambridge, 17, 43-4
Wash, the, 38
Water Newton hoard, 114-15
Wat's Dyke, 51
Wayland's Smithy, *21*
wells, 23, 24, 25, 109-12
Westness, Rousay, 18
White Tower, 32
Wild Edric of the Marches, 51-2
William I, the Conqueror, 32, 52
Wilsford Shaft, 22-5
Windover Hill, Sussex, 44
Winnall, Hants, 18
Wishart, George, 76
Woden, 47
Wookey Hole, 88-90